# STATE v. DIAMOND

## Problems and Case File

# NITA Educational Services Committee
# 1997

# STATE v. DIAMOND

by

**James H. Seckinger**
**Professor of Law**
**University of Notre Dame**

**Revised Fourth Edition**
**1992**

NATIONAL INSTITUTE FOR TRIAL ADVOCACY

Seckinger, James H. *State v. Diamond, Problems and Case File*, Revised Fourth Edition, (NITA, 1992).

ISBN 1-55681-315-5

1/96

# SECTION ONE

# PROBLEMS

# STATE v. DIAMOND
## Problems

## Table of Contents

# INTRODUCTION

The problems in this book are intended to simulate realistic courtroom situations. Advance preparation is essential to their successful utilization as instructional materials.

These problems refer to *State v. Diamond*, one of the case files in NITA's *Problems and Cases in Trial Advocacy, Law School Edition*, series. These case files have been designed to simulate the materials a trial lawyer would have on the eve of trial. The materials must be mastered before attempting to perform the problems in a courtroom setting.

All years in these materials are stated in the following form:

* YR-0 indicates the actual year in which the case is being tried (i.e., the present year);
* YR-1 indicates the next preceding year (please use the actual year);
* YR-2 indicates the second preceding year (please use the actual year); etc.

At the outset we should acknowledge that it is impossible for one person to teach another how to become a trial lawyer. Advocacy is an art, the performance of which is dependent on talent and mastery of skills. One becomes a trial lawyer through a mixture of predisposition, motivation, observation, doing it, reading how others have done it and then constantly repeating the latter three—doing, observing, and reading.

It is possible, however, to simulate some of the intellectual, ethical, emotional, and physical demands of trial lawyering and advocacy teaching in a mock courtroom or classroom setting. That is what is done at the National Institute for Trial Advocacy. These materials are intended to serve as the basic teaching materials for trial advocacy courses and programs that are based upon the learning-by-doing method. Although the materials have been prepared especially for NITA programs, they are adaptable for use in other settings.

Most of the skills learned in a trial advocacy course will be applicable to trial work generally, without regard to the nature of the case. Obviously, however, different kinds of cases present different problems. We believe that these materials illustrate some of the more significant peculiarities of business contract litigation.

The student should read the assigned case file as soon as possible. A reading of the complete case file early will permit the student to fit an individual problem into the context of the entire litigation. The student should then read the assigned problems and do as much preparation as possible in advance of the program. Preparation time during the program will be limited. Thus, advance preparation will allow a more efficient use of the limited time available during the program.

# METHOD OF INSTRUCTION

NITA programs, and other learning-by-doing programs, have certain unique characteristics to which these materials are particularly suited. These programs typically use teaching teams comprised of law teachers, practicing trial lawyers and judges. The programs are highly intensive, all-day sessions lasting from five to sixteen working days. All make substantial use of videotape to record student performances for later playback and critique.

These materials also are adaptable for the more typical law school program in which classes are spread out over a semester, teaching teams are unavailable and videotape may not be feasible. The following are some ideas for use of the materials whether they are used at an intensive NITA-type session or in a longer law school program.

It is contemplated that the materials will be used in a simulated courtroom session. A judge, whether actual or portrayed, will preside at the front of the classroom. A student lawyer will be called on to begin the problem. The examining lawyer will be opposed by an adversary, who will be portrayed by another member of the class or, when a teaching team is available, by a visiting lawyer. The witness will have been prepared and will respond to a proper examination. The lawyer may complete the examination or be interrupted so that another lawyer can continue the examination. Several lawyers may be called on to represent both sides before the problem is exhausted and the next problem begun.

At a NITA session, a section of twenty-four students will remain together for two hours to work on a series of problems. The section then ordinarily will split into two or three smaller groups. The students will continue to work on the problems in these groups.

During the course of any presentation by a student, whether in large or small groups, another lawyer may be called on to substitute for the participating lawyer. The substituting lawyer may pick up where the other left off or, with permission of the instructor, may begin again. In short, the students may be called on at any time to undertake an assigned examination.

Many teachers require universal preparation; each student must be prepared to perform at least one side of each problem.

# DIRECT, CROSS, AND REDIRECT EXAMINATION

The ability to examine and oppose the examination of witnesses in open court in an adversary setting is the most basic skill of the trial lawyer. Yet, the most common criticism of trial lawyers is that they are unable to conduct proper, intelligent, and purposeful examinations and to oppose these examinations.

As with any skill, practice is the only sure way to achievement. The practice should be conducted with some guidelines in mind.

1. The purpose of any witness examination is to elicit information.

2. The basic format is an interrogative dialogue.

3. The witness is probably insecure. She is appearing in a strange environment and is expected to perform under strange rules. This is a handicap you must overcome on direct and an advantage you have (and may choose to exploit) on cross.

4. Your questions should be short, simple, and understandable to the witness, the judge, and the jury on both direct and cross examination.

    (a)    It is imperative that your audience—the judge and the jury—understand your question so that they reasonably can anticipate and comprehend the answer.

    (b)    On direct examination the insecurity or anxieties of the witness will be increased if she does not understand your questions.

    (c)    On cross examination the complex argumentative question provides a refuge for the witness to evade the point.

5. As a general proposition, you may not lead on direct except as to preliminary matters or to refresh the recollection of the witness. Both of these exceptions are discretionary with the judge.

6. In any event, on direct examination leading questions and the perfunctory answers they elicit are not persuasive.

7. On cross examination you may lead and you should do so. Control of the witness on cross is imperative.

8. At the outset of direct examination, have the witness introduce herself. Then, place her in the controversy on trial, and elicit the who, where, when, what, how, and why of the relevant information the witness has to offer. Then quit. Do not be repetitious.

9. If you know that the cross examination will elicit unfavorable information, consider the possible advantage of eliciting it during your direct examination.

10. Do not conduct a cross examination that does nothing other than afford the witness an opportunity to repeat her direct testimony.

    (a)     If there is nothing to be gained by cross examination, waive it.

    (b)     If you can accomplish something by cross examination, get to it. Organize your points and make them.

    (c)     Be cautious about cross examining on testimony elicited on direct that was favorable to your position. You may lose it.

    (d)     Be cautious about asking a question to which you do not know or cannot reasonably anticipate the answer. Be particularly cautious in those situations in which the only evidence on the point will be the unknown answer.

11. Listen to (do not assume) the answers of the witness. As an examiner on either direct or cross examination, you are entitled to responsive answers. Insist on them by a gentle nudge on direct or a motion to strike on cross (unless, of course, the answer is favorable, in which event accept it and return to the pending question).

12. Objections to the form of the question must be made before an answer is given. If the question reveals that the answer sought will be inadmissible, an objection must precede the answer. The grounds of the objection should be succinctly and specifically stated. If the question does not reveal the potential inadmissibility of the answer, but the answer is inadmissible, a prompt motion to strike should be succinctly and specifically stated. Only the interrogator is entitled to move to strike an answer on the *sole* ground that it was unresponsive to the question. If the answer is unresponsive *and* contains objectionable matter, then the opposing counsel is entitled to object.

13. If an objection to the content of the answer (e.g., relevancy, hearsay, etc.) as opposed to the form of the question, is sustained, then the interrogator should consider the need for an offer of proof at the first available opportunity. If an objection to the form of the question is sustained, then the interrogator should rephrase the question to cure the objection.

Diamond Problems

# PROBLEM 1

## Sgt. Benbrook

Assume that the case is at trial and the state's first witness is Sgt. E. A. Benbrook.

(a)  For the state, conduct a direct examination of Sgt. Benbrook.

(b)  For the defendant, conduct a cross examination of Sgt. Benbrook.

(c)  For the state, conduct any necessary redirect examination.

# PROBLEM 2

## Beth Kelly

Assume that the case is at trial and the state has called Sgt. E.A. Benbrook.  The state's next witness is Beth Kelly.

(a)  For the state, conduct a direct examination of Ms. Kelly.

(b)  For the defendant, conduct a cross examination of Ms. Kelly.

(c)  For the state, conduct any necessary redirect examination.

## PROBLEM 3

### Estelle Mason

Assume that the case is at trial, the state has presented its case, and the defendant's motion for a judgment of acquittal has been denied. Assume further that John Diamond has testified in his own behalf. The defendant's next witness is Estelle Mason.

    (a)  For the defendant, conduct a direct examination of Ms. Mason.

    (b)  For the state, conduct a cross examination of Ms. Mason.

    (c)  For the defendant, conduct any necessary redirect examination.

## PROBLEM 4

### John Madden

Assume that the case is at trial, the state has presented its case, and the defendant's motion for a judgment of acquittal has been denied. Assume further that John Diamond and Estelle Mason have testified for the defense. The defendant's next witness is Officer John Madden.

    (a)  For the defendant, conduct a direct examination of Officer Madden.

    (b)  For the state, conduct a cross examination of Officer Madden.

    (c)  For the defendant, conduct any necessary redirect examination.

# HANDLING AND INTRODUCTION OF EXHIBITS

The ability to examine and oppose the examination of witnesses in open court in an adversary setting is the *most basic* skill of the trial lawyer.

The second basic skill of the trial lawyer is the proper, efficient, and orderly handling and introduction of tangible evidence. Again, however, a common criticism of the trial bar is its lack of facility in this truly simple undertaking.

This is all the more regrettable when one considers the highly persuasive quality of relevant exhibits. Jurors (and judges, too) trust them. They are the real thing. They do not exaggerate as witnesses do and they do not overstep their bounds as lawyers do. Many a case has been won or lost because a particularly intriguing exhibit was received in evidence or excluded.

The four touchstones for the handling and introduction of exhibits are:

1. Authenticity,

2. Relevance,

3. The Hearsay Rule, and

4. The Best Evidence Rule.

These four touchstones must be satisfied before an exhibit can be received in evidence. Some call it "laying the foundation." By whatever phrase, the essential element is testimony establishing that the exhibit is authentic and relevant and complies with both the hearsay and best evidence rules.

Authenticity is simply a demonstration that the exhibit is what it purports to be. Is this thing—whatever it is—that is being offered in evidence, *prima facie* that which it purports to be?[*] The essential requirement is testimonial vouching for the thing unless, of course, authenticity is established by admissions in the pleadings, discovery, or a request to admit. See, for example, Federal Rule of Civil Procedure 36.

---

[*]The standard is a prima facie showing of authenticity, as the court determines admissibility. The weight to be assigned to the particular piece of evidence is left to the fact finder.

Relevance, as well as the hearsay and best evidence rules, is intrinsically dependent on the issues raised in the case and the purpose for which the exhibit is offered in evidence. In each instance, however, the foundation must be laid demonstrating that the exhibit is relevant and that it complies with the hearsay and best evidence rules.

For each exhibit, counsel should check the four touchstones and then lay the foundation necessary for its admission in evidence through the testimony of one or more witnesses.

As in the case of witness examination, the skill of handling and introducing exhibits is developed by practice and is conducted with certain guidelines in mind.

1. Select with care the witness or witnesses you will use to lay the foundation for your exhibits. A mistake here could be fatal.

2. Because the introduction of exhibits usually is done through witnesses, keep in mind the basic principles of witness examination.

3. Have the exhibit marked for identification by the appropriate court official (usually the court reporter or clerk) at the earliest opportunity. Many lawyers have their exhibits marked for identification prior to trial in the sequence in which they expect to use them. Some judges insist on this. It is a good practice in cases involving many exhibits. But also consider the advantages to be gained from a brief pause (respite for the witness) and a little bit of the lawyer doing his "thing" that attends your stepping to the bench and requesting in a voice the jury can hear, "Your Honor, may the reporter mark this document (or object) defendant's exhibit 1 for identification?"

4. Once the exhibit has been marked for identification, include that identification in any reference you make to the exhibit and see to it that your opponent, the witnesses, and the judge do likewise. Never permit the record to read merely, "this letter" or "that bottle" or "the photograph," etc.

5. Proceed to "lay the foundation" as follows:

   (a) Elicit from the authenticating witness those facts that qualify him or her to authenticate the exhibit. For example, have the witness say he saw the gun in the robber's hand.

(b)     Have the witness identify the exhibit by saying, for example, that State's Exhibit 1 is the gun (or looks like the gun) the witness saw in the robber's hand.

(c)     If the condition of the exhibit is a factor in its relevancy, either elicit testimony that its condition has not changed between the event and the time of trial, or offer a testimonial explanation of the change in condition.

(d)     If the exhibit is a reproduction of a place, a thing, or an event (e.g., a photograph or a tape recording), elicit testimony that it fairly and accurately portrays that which it purports to portray.

(e)     If more than one witness is required to authenticate or connect the exhibit, withhold your offer until you have completed your foundation. A premature offer and rejection can condition a judge to reject the exhibit later when the foundation has been completed.

6.  Once the foundation for an exhibit has been laid properly, offer it in evidence and obtain a ruling on its admissibility. In some jurisdictions an exhibit may not be offered during cross examination, and in those instances the formal offer of the exhibit is reserved to your case in chief or rebuttal.

7.  When you are opposing the introduction of an exhibit, you are entitled to conduct a cross examination on the foundation before the court rules on the offer. The scope of this cross examination, often referred to as a voir dire on the exhibit, is limited to the admissibility of the exhibit. The proponent of the exhibit should be alert to so limit the voir dire on the exhibit and not permit the opponent to conduct a general cross examination on the weight that is to be given to the exhibit.

8.  When you are opposing the introduction of exhibits, be on the alert for changed conditions and distortions (particularly in photographs). Insist that an adequate testimonial explanation of the changes be given by the authenticating witness.

9.  Do not permit your opponent to display tangible items in the presence of the jury until they are marked for identification and proffered to the witness for identification.

10. Keep a separate record of the status of your exhibits and those of your opponent. Know at all times their identification numbers, their general descriptions, the witness or witnesses who authenticated them, and whether they have been offered and received or excluded. Many lawyers keep a columnar record somewhat like this:

### Plaintiff's Exhibits

| No. | Description | Witness | Date or page of record offered | Date or page of record received | Date or page of record refused |
|---|---|---|---|---|---|
| 1. | Letter from Jones | Smith | 6/1/88 p. 138 | 6/1/88 p. 140 | |
| 2. | Hammer | Jones | 6/2/88 p. 100 | | 6/2/88 p. 210 |

11. At the close of your case, if you are uncertain as to the status of any of your exhibits, reoffer them before you rest.

Each exhibit has its own standards of authenticity and admissibility. For our purposes, they are better demonstrated than described.

# PROBLEM 5

## Gun, Cartridges, Cigarette Pack

(a) For the state, introduce into evidence the gun, the two cartridges, and the cigarette pack that were found in the vestibule of the Truck Stop Cafe after Ms. Doyle was shot. Prepare exhibits consistent with the information in the case file.

You may use any witness or witnesses you desire to lay the foundation for the exhibits. Examine the witness(es) to the extent necessary to lay the foundation and then offer the exhibits. Be prepared to discuss your choice of witness(es).

(b) For the defendant, oppose the examination of the witness(es) and the offer of the exhibits. Be prepared to voir dire the witness(es) on the admissibility of the exhibits.

# PROBLEM 6

## Bullet

(a) For the state, introduce into evidence the bullet that was removed from the body of Ms. Doyle. Prepare an exhibit consistent with the information in the case file.

You may use any witness or witnesses you desire to lay the foundation for the exhibit. Examine the witness(es) to the extent necessary to lay the foundation and then offer the exhibit. Be prepared to discuss your choice of witness(es).

(b) For the defendant, oppose the examination of the witness(es) and the offer of the exhibit. Be prepared to voir dire the witness(es) on the admissibility of the exhibit.

## *Note on Chain of Custody*

Just as important as the ability to examine witnesses with regard to real evidence is the ability to set up procedures for maintaining a chain of custody when such a chain is necessary. Cases may be lost because the party offering evidence has used sloppy procedures prior to trial. The next two problems are intended to give you practice not only in examining witnesses, but also in protecting evidence through the maintenance of a chain of custody. On the opponent's side, the problems should demonstrate the opportunities for objection to certain kinds of real evidence.

## PROBLEM 7

### Hospital Record

(a) For the defendant, introduce into evidence the hospital record relating to Ms. Doyle's admission and treatment. You may use any witness or witnesses you desire to lay the foundation for the exhibit. Examine the witness(es) to the extent necessary to lay the foundation and then offer the exhibit. Be prepared to discuss your choice of witness(es).

(b) For the state, oppose the examination of the witness(es) and the offer of the exhibit. Be prepared to voir dire the witness(es) on the admissibility of the exhibit.

# PROBLEM 8

## Diagram

Assume that the case is at trial.

Prepare a diagram of the Truck Stop Cafe that is large enough to be seen by a jury. (See the diagram in the case file.) Add to the diagram the following:

1. Position of the defendant when he was sitting in the cafe, his path to the vestibule, and his position when he was standing in the vestibule at the time the shots were fired.

2. Positions of Beth Kelly, Joseph Foster, and Estelle Mason in the cafe at the time the shots were fired.

3. Any other items that you think would be helpful to the jury.

(a) For the state, conduct a direct examination of any witness or witnesses you choose, and either introduce the diagram as demonstrative evidence or use it as a demonstrative aid. Be prepared to discuss your choice of witness(es).

(b) For the defendant, oppose the introduction or use of the diagram and conduct a cross examination of the witness(es).

# IMPEACHMENT AND REHABILITATION

## Impeachment

Although it is a part of the cross examiner's art, impeachment is a sufficiently difficult problem in itself to warrant separate consideration.

1. The cross examiner must consider not only how to impeach, but also whether the witness should be impeached at all. Just as the trial lawyer should not cross examine in some situations, he may often decide wisely that although impeaching evidence is available, it should not be used. If the witness has not hurt your case, usually it is better not to impeach and risk offending the jury. If the testimony of a witness can be turned to your advantage, as in the case of a truly impartial expert witness, do so and do not impeach.

2. Foundation for impeachment by prior inconsistent statement:

    (a)    Under the law of most jurisdictions, the witness must be confronted with a prior inconsistent statement during cross examination. If her attention has not been called to the earlier statement, extrinsic evidence of it will not be admissible. Cross examination should be specific as to the time, circumstances, and content of the earlier statement.

    (b)    The rule requiring a foundation for prior inconsistent statements is relaxed under the Federal Rules of Evidence. Federal Rule 613(b) provides that the witness must be "afforded an opportunity to explain or deny" the prior inconsistent statement in order for extrinsic evidence to be admissible, but no time sequence is specified. Therefore, as long as the witness is available to explain the inconsistency if she so desires, extrinsic proof is admissible.

    (c)    Most advocates will prefer to lay a foundation on cross examination irrespective of whether or not it is required under the rules. The reason for this is twofold. First, the witness may admit the statement, making extrinsic evidence unnecessary. More significantly, confronting a witness with her own inconsistency often will have a dramatic impact that cannot be duplicated by introducing evidence of the earlier statement through another person.

3. If the witness denies making an earlier statement, be prepared to prove it by extrinsic evidence.

4.  If the witness admits making an inconsistent or otherwise impeaching statement, do not ask questions that give her an opportunity to explain it away, unless you are certain that that cannot be done. The attorney who has called the witness will have an opportunity on redirect examination to elicit explanations, if any are available. This affords you the opportunity for recross.

5.  There is no need, and it is usually harmful, to dwell on the impeaching matter after it has been brought out in cross examination. Remember, you have a closing argument.

## Rehabilitation

If a witness has been impeached during cross examination, counsel must evaluate whether to attempt to rehabilitate the witness on redirect examination.

1.  As with any redirect examination, counsel should limit the scope of the redirect to those items in which the witness needs an opportunity to explain or amplify upon her testimony after the cross examination. Redirect examination and rehabilitation of a witness is not the time to rehash the direct testimony once again.

2.  In considering whether to rehabilitate a witness on redirect examination, counsel should first of all be absolutely certain that the witness has, in fact, been impeached. If the witness has not been effectively impeached, do not attempt to rehabilitate the witness as you may only make matters worse.

3.  Rehabilitation generally consists of providing the witness with an opportunity to explain the circumstances pertaining to the impeachment and to elicit any "exculpatory" factors. Give the witness the opportunity to put the impeachment in context.

4.  If the impeachment can be explained, do it; if not, leave it alone on redirect as you just may make matters worse.

5.  If the witness has been impeached by a prior inconsistent statement, counsel should consider the admissibility of any prior consistent statements. See 801(d)(1)(B) of the Federal Rules of Evidence. Prior consistent statements are generally admissible if they rebut an express or implied charge of recent fabrication.

# PROBLEM 9

## Beth Kelly

Assume that Beth Kelly testified on direct examination as follows:

I saw Diamond step in front of her. He blocked her way into the cafe. I heard voices—mostly Diamond's. Then I saw Diamond reach into his belt. I heard a shot. I heard Trudi scream and then another shot. I then saw her fall to the floor.

Assume further that the rest of her direct testimony followed her statement in the case file.

(a) For the defendant, conduct a cross examination and impeachment of Ms. Kelly.

(b) For the state, conduct any necessary redirect examination.

Diamond Problems

# WITNESS PREPARATION

Chronologically, this topic should precede all that has gone before.  As other teachers of trial advocacy have observed, however, exposure to the pitfalls of the courtroom sharpens the trial lawyer's awareness of the need for thorough witness preparation.  (See, for example, the sequence of exercises in A. Levin and H. Cramer, *Trial Advocacy, Problems and Materials*, Foundation Press, 1968.) Hopefully, that has been the case here.

From a coaching standpoint, this topic might well be eliminated.  In the privacy of a lawyer's office, there are no rules of  evidence to restrain the preparation and examination of witnesses.  Further, when one multiplies the lawyer types by the myriad of witness types, the number of combinations is infinite.  Thus, it is impossible to actually teach witness preparation.

A great deal has been written on the subject.  There are a variety of common sense admonitions calculated to put a witness in the most favorable and persuasive posture:  be at ease; don't chew gum on the stand; dress neatly and conservatively; listen to the question and don't answer it until it is completed; don't worry about where counsel is going on direct or cross examination; just answer the questions.

There are, however, some questions about witness preparation and some problems which recur with remarkable frequency that should be raised.  The following problems are intended to illustrate them.  As you confront them, keep in mind that our English brothers at the bar seldom encounter them, for in England it is regarded as unethical for the barrister to "woodshed" the witness.

## PROBLEM 10

## John Diamond

The case is scheduled for trial in one week. Your partner was just called out of town on an emergency. He asked you to handle the final preparations for trial and said he would be back a day or so before the trial begins. He asked you to see Diamond to make sure he is ready for trial and to prepare him for his testimony.

Interview Mr. Diamond and prepare him for trial.

# ADVANCED DIRECT AND CROSS EXAMINATION

## PROBLEM 11

### John Diamond

Assume that the state has presented its case and that the defendant's motion for judgment of acquittal has been denied. The defense calls John Diamond as its first witness.

(a) For the defendant, conduct a direct examination of Mr. Diamond.

(b) For the state, conduct a cross examination of Mr. Diamond.

(c) For the defendant, conduct any necessary redirect examination.

## PROBLEM 12

### Kelly, Foster, and Mason

The purpose of this exercise is to develop a theme or trial strategy and implement it through the examination of the witnesses. Assume that Beth Kelly, Joseph Foster, and Estelle Mason will testify on direct examination consistent with their prior statements. Since the statements of the witnesses are set out in the case file, and, for the purposes of conserving time, there will be no direct examination, the trial strategy will be developed through cross and redirect examinations.

(a) For the defendant, conduct cross examinations of Ms. Kelly and Mr. Foster.

(b) For the state, conduct redirect examinations of Ms. Kelly and Mr. Foster.

(c) For the state, conduct a cross examination of Ms. Mason.

(d) For the defendant, conduct a redirect examination of Ms. Mason.

(e) For the state, what would be the principal points raised in your closing argument with respect to the eyewitness testimony?

(f) For the defendant, what would be the principal points raised in your closing argument with respect to the eyewitness testimony?

Diamond Problems

# EXAMINATION OF EXPERT WITNESSES

Conservatively, eighty percent of all trials in courts of general jurisdiction involve the examination of skilled or expert witnesses. For example, in personal injury cases, there are medical experts and experts in accident reconstruction; in criminal cases, there are chemical, ballistics, fingerprint, and handwriting experts; and in commercial cases, there are economists and market analysts. The opportunities for using expert witnesses are limited only by human knowledge and the trial lawyer's ingenuity. Accordingly, no lawyer is worthy of the name "trial lawyer" until he or she has mastered the techniques that attend the direct and cross examination of expert witnesses.

The function of the expert witness is to bring to the trial of a case knowledge beyond the ken of the average layman and to apply that knowledge to the facts in the case so that jurors may better determine the issues.

The basic guidelines are stated simply, but they are not so simple to apply:

1. **Qualifications.** The proposed expert witness must be qualified by training and/or experience in a recognized field of knowledge that is beyond the ken of the average layman.[*]

2. **Explanation of Expertise.** If the field of knowledge is at all esoteric, the expert witness should provide a brief explanation of it, particularly with reference to its application to the case at hand.

3. **Ruling on Qualifications as an Expert.** In some jurisdictions, after the witness' qualifications have been elicited, the witness is tendered to the court as an expert in his or her field, and the court either accepts or rejects the witness as an expert at that time. Some courts, however, are reluctant to give their imprimatur to the witness' testimony or to rule on the witness' qualifications as an expert prior to hearing the actual opinion the expert will be asked to give. In those jurisdictions, the direct examination simply proceeds unless there is an objection, at which time the court rules.

4. **Cross Examination on Qualifications.** The opposing counsel may voir dire (cross examine) the witness on his or her qualifications at the time the witness is tendered to the court as an expert witness or, if that procedure is not used, before the witness is permitted to express his or her opinion.

---

[*]Under the Federal Rules of Evidence, the test is whether the witness' knowledge, training, or experience will assist the trier of fact in understanding the evidence or determining a fact in issue. Note also that the witness, if qualified as an expert, may testify in the form of an opinion or otherwise. F.R.E. 702.

5. **Basis of Opinion.** The direct examination should elicit a description of what the expert did with regard to the case, and the facts that are the basis of the opinion.[*]

The facts that may be used as the basis for the expert's opinion and elicited on direct examination are limited to those facts that

(a)     the expert personally observed,

(b)     were elicited in the courtroom and heard by the expert, or

(c)     were transmitted to the expert hypothetically.

In the federal courts and some state courts, facts that were made known to the expert outside of court and other than by his or her own perception also may be used if they are of a type reasonably relied upon by experts in the expert's field. F.R.E. 703.

In most state courts, the hearsay rule and the other traditional principles of admissibility apply to expert testimony. Opposing counsel should keep an ear carefully tuned for the application of these principles during the expert's direct examination. In the federal courts and some state courts that have relaxed the hearsay rule and the other traditional requirements for admissibility for expert testimony, the expert may testify to, and base his or her opinion on, facts that are not admissible in evidence.

---

[*]In most state courts the direct examination <u>must</u> elicit the factual basis for the expert's opinion as a foundation prerequisite for the expert's stating an opinion. This is the method for ensuring that the expert's opinion is based on admissible evidence.

While in federal courts the underlying facts for the expert's opinion need not be disclosed on direct examination, the expert will be required to disclose them on cross examination. F.R.E. 705. The court, however, has the discretion to require that the underlying facts be disclosed prior to the expert's stating his or her opinion when the interests of justice so require. See also F.R.E. 703, which says the expert's opinion need not be based on admissible evidence.

The underlying facts for the expert's opinion are usually quite persuasive, and most trial lawyers will make them integral parts of their direct examinations. The trial lawyer has the option in federal court, and her or she may tailor the direct examination to meet the needs of the particular case.

6. **Opinion.** The expert's opinion cannot be speculation or conjecture. Rather, it must be an opinion to a reasonable degree of certainty within the expert's field. Most courts require that the opinion by elicited in a two-question sequence: (1) Do you have an opinion as to——?, and then (2) What is that opinion? This gives the opposing counsel an opportunity to object before the opinion is heard by the jury.

When the expert's opinion is based on facts that the expert did not personally observe or hear in the courtroom, the hypothetical-question format is required in most state courts. However, in the federal courts and some state courts, the hypothetical question is no longer required, and the trial lawyer has the option of using it or not. F.R.E. 703, 705. When this format is optional, the trial lawyer's decision is a matter of trial strategy, which depends on many factors. Perhaps we will see some of those factors demonstrated in the exercises.

The primary objections that are available to opposing counsel when the hypothetical-question format is used are:

(a)    That the hypothetical question included facts not in evidence, or

(b)    That it did not include relevant facts that are in evidence.

Thus, in a complicated case the hypothetical question can be quite cumbersome. In anything but the most routine case it can be a delicate procedure with pitfalls to snare the unwary.

7. **Cross Examination.** The expert witness may be cross examined with respect to his or her opinion on the basis of:

(a)    The expert's qualifications;[*]

(b)    Other facts in the case; or

(c)    The published opinions of other recognized authorities in the field (learned treatises).

---

[*]The cross examination of qualifications, discussed in paragraph 4, is a voir dire on the admissibility of the expert's opinion. The cross examination here goes to the weight of the expert's opinion. Counsel should weigh carefully whether to cross examine in both instances, or to elect one or the other.

Diamond Problems

# PROBLEM 13

## Dr. James Pierce

The state calls Dr. James Pierce for the purpose of establishing cause of death and the paths of the bullets.

   (a)   For the state, conduct a direct examination of Dr. Pierce.

   (b)   For the defendant, conduct a cross examination of Dr. Pierce.

   (c)   For the state, conduct any necessary redirect examination.

Diamond Problems

**SECTION TWO**

**CASE FILE**

# STATE v. DIAMOND
## Case File

### Table of Contents

# INTRODUCTION

A grand jury has charged John Diamond with first degree murder in the shooting death of Trudi Doyle on December 1, YR-1, at the Truck Stop Cafe on Highway 33 outside of Nita City.

Mr. Diamond and Ms. Doyle had been living together for two months immediately prior to her death. Ms. Doyle was a waitress at the Truck Stop Cafe, and Mr. Diamond was a police officer with the Nita City Police Department. Both Ms. Doyle and Mr. Diamond worked night shifts.

On the morning of December 1, YR-1, Mr. Diamond went to the Truck Stop Cafe to meet Ms. Doyle when she got off work at 6:00 A.M. He had just resigned from the police force and had left a California forwarding address at the station. Mr. Diamond entered the cafe and sat in a booth. Ms. Doyle was sitting in a booth at the other side of the cafe talking with other waitresses. She did not speak to Mr. Diamond, and then at 6:30 A.M., Ms. Doyle got up from the booth and went to the vestibule in the front of the cafe. Mr. Diamond followed her and they talked for a few minutes. A shot rang out, followed by a second shot. Ms. Doyle slumped to the floor and died within minutes. Mr. Diamond remained at the scene and was arrested when the police arrived.

The applicable law is contained in the statutes and the proposed jury instructions set forth at the end of the file.

All years in these materials are stated in the following form:

YR-0    indicates the actual year in which the case is being tried (i.e., the present year);
YR-1    indicates the next preceding year (please use the actual year);
YR-2    indicates the second preceding year (please use the actual year), etc.

# SPECIAL INSTRUCTIONS FOR USE AS A FULL TRIAL

When this case file is used for a full trial, the following witnesses may be called by the parties:

State:     E.A. Benbrook
            Beth Kelly
            Joseph Foster
            Dr. James Pierce

Defense:  John Diamond
            John Madden
            Estelle Mason

A party need not call all of the witnesses listed as its witnesses. With the exception of the defendant, who may be called only by the defense, any or all of the witnesses may be called by either party. However, if a witness is to be called by a party other than the one for whom he or she is listed, the party for whom the witness is listed will select and prepare the witness.

Required Stipulations:

1. Neutron activation tests of John Diamond's right hand were positive.

2. Neutron activation tests of Trudi Doyle's hands were negative.

3. Tests of powder burns on Trudi Doyle's jacket were inconclusive due to extensive bleeding.

4. Blood on the jacket was type O negative. Trudi Doyle has type O negative blood.

5. Comparison of bullet found in Trudi Doyle's body with bullet fired from John Diamond's gun shows that both were fired from that gun.

6. The gun was fingerprinted, but no usable prints were found.

7. The gun has a trigger pull of six pounds. This is an average pull, midway between a hair trigger and a heavy trigger pull.

8. When fired, the gun recoils approximately 15 degrees.

9. The Memorial Hospital medical record was made and kept in the regular course of the hospital's business. William Coleman, the medical records librarian, would so testify if called as a witness.

10. The transcript of the statement given by John Diamond is authentic.

## IN THE CIRCUIT COURT OF
## DARROW COUNTY, NITA

THE PEOPLE OF THE STATE OF NITA          )
                                         )
                    v.                   )          Case No. CR1473
                                         )
JOHN DIAMOND,                            )          INDICTMENT
Defendant.                               )

   The Grand Jury in and for the county of Darrow, State of Nita,
upon their oath and in the name and by the authority of the State
of Nita, does hereby charge the following offense under the
Criminal Code of the State of Nita:

   That on December 1, YR-1, at and within the County of Darrow
in the State of Nita, John Diamond committed the crime of

### MURDER IN THE FIRST DEGREE

in violation of Section 18-3-102 of the Nita Criminal Code of
1974, as amended, in that he, after deliberation and with the
intent to cause the death of a person other than himself, caused
the death of Trudi Doyle with a deadly weapon, namely a Mauser
automatic pistol.

   Contrary to the form of the Statute and against the peace and
dignity of the People of the State of Nita.


                         A TRUE BILL:


                         _Jeanne Mitchell_
                         Foreperson of the Grand Jury

_Paul R. Roberts_
Paul R. Roberts
District Attorney
Darrow County
State of Nita   99995
(721) 555-3884


DATED: December 15, YR-1

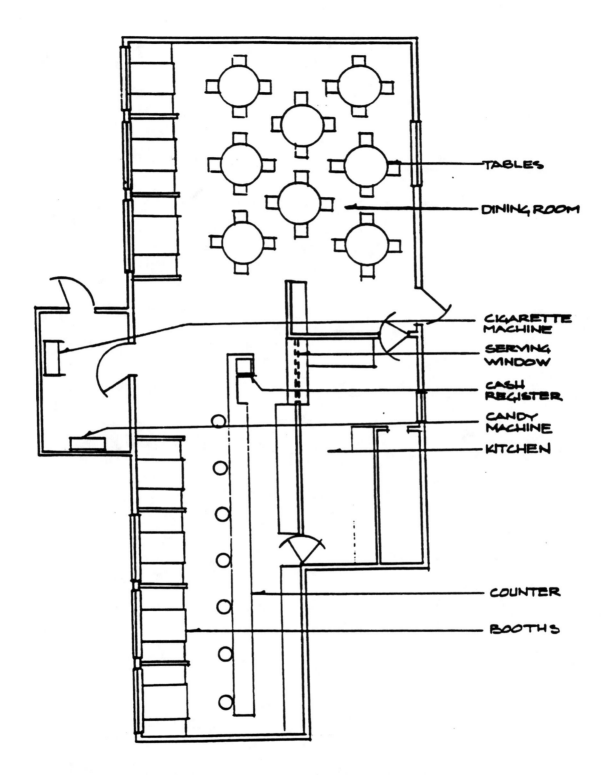

TABLES

DINING ROOM

CIGARETTE MACHINE

SERVING WINDOW

CASH REGISTER

CANDY MACHINE

KITCHEN

COUNTER

BOOTHS

DIAGRAM OF <u>TRUCK STOP CAFE</u>
HIGHWAY 33, NITA CITY

(NOT DRAWN TO SCALE)

Diamond Case File

## NITA CITY POLICE DEPARTMENT
## OFFENSE REPORT

Re:                    Trudi Doyle

Location:              Truck Stop Cafe
                       Highway 33
                       Nita City, Nita

Offense:               Homicide

Date of Report:        December 9, YR-1

By:                    Sgt. E.A. Benbrook
                       Homicide Division


On December 1, YR-1, at about 6:55 a.m., I received a telephone call that there had been a shooting at the Truck Stop Cafe. I went immediately to the cafe. When I arrived, I met Officers Johnson and Preston who also had just arrived. I instructed Officers Johnson and Preston to secure the scene and check for witnesses in the cafe.

Upon checking the scene, I saw Trudi Doyle lying in the vestibule of the cafe, and Johnny Diamond was kneeling next to her holding her hand, with a handgun by his side. There was blood on the front of her jacket, and she appeared to be dead--her eyes were open, but she didn't move at all. I didn't touch the body or check to determine if she was, in fact, dead.

After seeing Ms. Doyle lying there and Diamond kneeling next to her, I picked up the gun and said to Diamond, "All right Diamond, what happened?" He didn't say anything, he just kind of stared off into space. I said "let's go" or something like that and then he got up. I took him to the police car, handcuffed him, and placed him in the back of the car. I told him he was under arrest for investigation of assault, or homicide if she were dead, and advised him of his Miranda rights--to remain silent and to have a lawyer. (I read the rights off of our departmental card that we carry.) He didn't say anything or respond at all. He just calmly sat there in the car. He looked normal and appeared to understand and know everything that was going on. I then left the car and instructed Officer Preston to stand at the rear of the car while I continued the investigation.

The coroner arrived and pronounced Ms. Doyle dead. Her body was transferred to the County Morgue for an autopsy by Deputy Coroner Dr. Pierce.

Ms. Doyle was found lying in the vestibule or entranceway to the Truck Stop Cafe. It is a glass-enclosed structure nine feet wide by twelve feet long (inside measurements). The lower four feet of the walls are wood and the rest is glass. Both doors are glass. I found a package of Winston cigarettes (unopened) on the floor next to Ms. Doyle. I first saw it when Ms. Doyle's body was being moved out of the vestibule. The package was partially covered by Ms. Doyle's legs. There was no blood on it. Two expended cartridges were found in the northeast corner of the vestibule. A mutilated bullet was lodged in the west wall 14" to the south of the cigarette machine, 30" above the floor. I marked the cartridges with my initials, placed the cartridges and the package of Winstons in an evidence envelope, and then placed the envelope in an evidence locker at the station.

I spoke with Beth Kelly, who was identified by Officer Johnson as an eyewitness. She told me that Ms. Doyle had gone to get cigarettes and Mr. Diamond had intercepted her in the vestibule, that she saw Ms. Doyle shake her head "no," then two shots rang out, and Ms. Doyle slumped to the floor. At that time I didn't speak with the other two witnesses, Estelle Mason (a waitress) and Joe Foster (a local farmer), but simply got their names and addresses.

I checked on Diamond in the car once or twice during my investigation at the scene, and each time he was still calmly sitting in the car. I never saw him look over at Ms. Doyle, not even when the coroner came and examined her. After the coroner examined Ms. Doyle, I told Diamond that she was dead. He didn't respond at all, just calmly sat there like nothing had happened.

Officers Johnson and Preston took Diamond to the County Jail and he was booked for investigation of homicide. After the booking process, the lab performed a neutron activation test on Diamond's hands. The results were positive. The lab also performed a neutron activation test on Ms. Doyle's hands at the morgue. Results negative.

I retained custody of the handgun that I found next to Diamond and the body of Ms. Doyle. It was a Mauser-Werke, HSc, 7.65 mm. automatic, serial number D 08865. When I got back to the police department, I put my initials on the gun and placed it in an evidence locker. The evidence locker is in our custodian's office. I completed the forms for the custodian. There is always a person on duty at this office, and there is a ledger or receipt for signing articles in and out. That way we have a record of where things are at all times.

Mr. Diamond gave a statement on the day of the shooting, December 1, at approximately 3:30 p.m. The statement was given in the presence of myself, Officer James Anderson, and Donna Williams, a certified shorthand reporter.

On December 2, I checked out gun registration files and determined that the Mauser automatic had been registered to John Diamond in November, YR-2. All guns have to be registered, and records are kept in the police department with a central file for the state in Capitol City.

I then examined and test-fired the Mauser automatic. The gun was operable. I test-fired it into a special box designed for that purpose and then recovered the bullet. I had received a bullet from Dr. Pierce, deputy coroner, which was recovered from the body of Ms. Doyle. I compared the two bullets and determined that they had been fired from the same gun. This is determined by examining the bullets under a microscope and looking at the "lands" and "grooves". There were identical markings on both of the bullets. In order to be absolutely certain, I sent the bullets to the Nita State Crime Laboratory and requested their opinion. I received the bullets back with a letter signed by Mr. Michael J. Harvey, stating that he had examined them, that they had identical markings, and it was his opinion that they had been fired from the same gun. The bullet which had been recovered from the vestibule wall was too mutilated to permit comparison.

I have received special training in firearm testing and identification at the Nita State Crime Laboratory in Capitol City. This was about two years ago. I keep up-to-date on it by reading the material distributed by the Nita State Crime Laboratory and the FBI.

I submitted the jacket Ms. Doyle was wearing to the State Crime Laboratory for testing. Results on powder burns were inconclusive, due to the amount of blood on the jacket. Blood type same as Ms. Doyle. Two holes in the front of the jacket indicated that the holes were caused by bullets.

I knew John Diamond when he was a police officer with our department. He is thirty-three years old and he is a big man, over six feet tall and around 200 pounds. I first met John Diamond in November, YR-2, when he joined the force. I knew him fairly well, although I never worked with him. I would see him at the station quite often, and we talked about general topics. I found him pleasantly talkative, but not very revealing about his personal life. He did mention that he was married with two children, but that he had been separated from them for some time and was in the process of a divorce. He talked about his children a little but never about his ex-wife. He dated some girls occasionally and then he met Trudi Doyle. He would talk about her, although never with any specifics. The conversation would always be general, and just enough to know that he was with her.

I knew Ms. Doyle but only to recognize her, and that she worked as a waitress at the Truck Stop Cafe. I didn't know anything about her personal life.

On the day Ms. Doyle was shot, December 1, I was at the station and saw John Diamond. He came off duty from his shift at 5:30 a.m. I saw him as he came into the station, and he went back to his locker. As he was leaving I saw him, and we talked for a few minutes. He said that he had just turned in his resignation, and he was going to California to start over. I wished him good luck and kidded him about his love life. He said--"Well, wish me luck on that; I'm going to talk to her." I don't remember the exact words, but that was basically what he said.

When I was talking to him I noticed that he had his "off duty" gun in his waistband. I saw that the hammer was back and it was in the cocked position. I just assumed the safety was on, but I couldn't see it. It would be extremely hazardous to carry the gun cocked if the safety is off. I don't think it is unusual to carry a gun cocked with a round in the chamber, as long as the safety is on, especially for a police officer.

I talked to Diamond around 6:00 a.m. I got the call from the Truck Stop Cafe on the shooting around 6:55 a.m.

Submitted by: _E.A. Benbrook_____
Sgt. E.A. Benbrook*
Homicide Division
Nita City Police Department

---

*Editor's Note: Sgt. E.A. Benbrook has been a police officer with the Nita City Police Department for twelve years. He has been a sergeant for four years and has been in charge of the homicide division for two years. He is married with two children.

# NITA CITY POLICE DEPARTMENT

## STATEMENT OF BETH KELLY[1]

My name is Beth Kelly.  I am a short-order cook at the Truck Stop Cafe, working the day shift from 6:00 a.m. until 2:30 p.m. I live at 405 1/2 South Fourth Street, Nita City.  I am twenty-six, single, and live by myself.

I knew Trudi Doyle when she worked at the Truck Stop Cafe with me, and also when she lived with me for about six months.  I also knew John Diamond.  He used to come into the Truck Stop Cafe a lot, and then he began dating Trudi.  At the time of her death, Trudi was twenty-three years old and had been working as a waitress at the Truck Stop Cafe since sometime in March, YR-1. She was married and had a little boy, but was in the process of divorcing her husband.  She had been separated from her husband since she came to Nita City and began working in the cafe.  John Diamond is in his early thirties.  He was married with two children, but was separated from his wife and children.  Trudi told me that his divorce had been pending for some time.

On December 1, YR-1, I arrived at work on time, as usual.  In fact, I always arrive between 5:30 and 5:45 a.m.  When I walked in, I saw Trudi Doyle and two or three other waitresses who were coming off their shift.  They went to a booth on the north side of the cafe and had some coffee.  After a little while I got my first order of the day, hotcakes.  I remember this because when I went to the serving window to get the order, I could see Trudi get up from the booth and walk toward the front door.  I turned back around and saw that she had gotten some cigarettes from the machine in the vestibule, and that Johnny Diamond was also standing in the vestibule, but with his back to the door, blocking her way back in the cafe.  He must have been sitting in a back booth.  I didn't see him get up and walk over the vestibule.

Trudi was facing me, and Diamond was in front of her with his back toward me.  Trudi had a pack of cigarettes in her left hand. It was a red and white package, the size of a cigarette pack. She smoked Winstons and she would always go the vestibule and get them from the machine there.

It looked like they were about to have a fight, if you know what I mean, from the way Diamond sort of stepped in front of her to block her path to the door and by the way she shook her head

---

[1]This statement was given to Sgt. E.A. Benbrook at the Truck Stop Cafe on December 4, YR-1.

"no" when he asked her something. I couldn't hear what was being said since they were in the vestibule, but I did see her shake her head "no." I could see pretty well because it is glass-enclosed, and also the door is all glass. I was only fifteen feet or so away from them, the serving window being six to eight feet behind the cash register. The next thing I knew I heard a shot and saw some smoke. Trudi screamed, throwing her hand over her heart, and I thought, "Oh, God, he shot her." I started for the back thinking I should call the police, but I saw the dishwasher had fainted so I stopped to help her. Then I heard a second shot. It was a few seconds later, five to ten seconds.

By the time I came out to the front of the cafe, Trudi was lying on the floor, and he was kneeling next to her holding her hand. I grabbed a wet rag and went back to help revive the dishwasher. When I came back to the front the police had come, and they took Diamond to the police car. I talked to Sgt. Benbrook and told him what I saw.

I have seen Diamond in the cafe before and knew it was him as soon as I saw him that morning on December 1. He usually came in early to have breakfast and pick up Trudi as she came off her shift. I would have no trouble identifying him if I saw him again.

Trudi didn't have a gun that morning or at anytime that I know about. She had a small purse and when she went to the vestibule she left it in the booth. The dress she wore as a waitress had one pocket in it. She had the guest checks, cigarettes, and tips in it. No, it wasn't big enough to hold a gun. Regarding guns, she did say once or twice that Diamond was teaching her how to shoot a gun--target practice--and something about knowing how to use a gun for her protection. Well, it looks now as though she needed that kind of protection, especially against him.

Trudi was right-handed. I often saw her writing on the orders and checks for the customers.

I knew Trudi. We talked at the cafe, and also she lived with me for about six months before she moved in with Diamond. We were pretty good friends, and she was good company for me. She talked to me about her relationship with Diamond, and also about her former husband. He was certainly no good--he drank a lot and would beat her up. She was very happy to have gotten out of that situation. She had one child, a boy around two, and she talked about him often. He was living with her mother in Capitol City. Of course she worried a lot about these problems, but she seemed to be handling everything all right and never got too upset or depressed about them.

Diamond wanted to go West, and he wanted Trudi to go with him. But she couldn't make up her mind, and she seemed reluctant. We talked about it four or five times the last two or three days before she was killed. She liked Diamond, but she didn't know if she wanted to settle down again so soon. She was worried about getting into another bad relationship. She said that she thought she loved Diamond, but wasn't sure.

I think she must have decided not to go with Diamond and when she told him "no" he shot her. He must have wanted her awful bad.

The first time I saw them together in the cafe that morning was when they were in the vestibule. Trudi had been sitting with the other waitresses before she got up to get the cigarettes. Diamond must have been sitting someplace else by himself. She did not go talk to him--he went after her.

There were about ten to fifteen people in the cafe at the time Trudi was shot. There were a few people at the counter and the rest were in the booths.

I have read the above statement consisting of three pages, and it is true and correct.


Signed: *Beth Kelly*          Date: ____12-4-YR-1____
        Beth Kelly


Witness: *Ed Benbrook*          Date: ____12-4-YR-1____
        Sgt. Benbrook
        Nita City Police Department

# NITA CITY POLICE DEPARTMENT

## STATEMENT OF JOSEPH FOSTER[2]

My name is Joseph Foster. I am a farmer, living on the outskirts of Nita City. Three or four times a week, I drive my truck into town for supplies. I do this after my early morning chores and usually stop at the Truck Stop Cafe for breakfast on the way. On December 1, YR-1, the day of the shooting, I had done just that and entered the cafe at about 6:15 or 6:20 a.m. I sat at the counter and Estelle Mason waited on me, as usual. I ordered my hotcakes and orange juice like I do every time I'm there. I was sitting at the counter, one seat over from the cash register.

I don't know any of the other waitresses by name, but I noticed a group of them—three or four—sitting in a booth, far to my left, when I first walked in. The place wasn't very crowded yet, and I guess they were taking a coffee break 'til business picked up.

After ordering, I just sat there making conversation with Estelle, who was busy cleaning up the counter where I was sitting. Several seconds went by when a fella came tearing down the aisle to my right. He must've been sitting at one of the booths in that area of the restaurant, but I hadn't noticed him 'til then. He seemed to be in a big hurry and walked right past me to the front door which I had my back to. I turned around when he reached the door to see why he was in such a hurry. One of the waitresses was standing in the entrance vestibule at the cigarette machine. She got some cigarettes, turned, and was coming back inside. The fella went into the vestibule, and the glass door shut behind him. I could see they were talking, but couldn't hear what they were saying. He was a lot bigger than she, and so all I could see of her was her head. Although I do remember seeing her hand up in the air with some cigarettes in it about as high as her head and about 1 to 1½ feet from her head. It was her hand that was closest to me, that would be her right hand. I couldn't see her other hand. I started to turn around and was about to say something to Estelle when I heard a shot fired in the vestibule. I immediately hit the floor to my right as my war instincts told me; I had fought in Korea. A few seconds later another shot rang out. I'd say it was a good five to six seconds before the second was fired.

---

[2]This statement was given to Officer Preston at Mr. Foster's farm on December 3, YR-1.

When I was sure all the shooting was finished, I moved toward the vestibule slowly and saw the man kneeling next to the waitress, holding her hand. She had obviously been shot, and there was blood all over. A gun was lying on the floor near both of them. The people at the cafe said the lady was Trudi Doyle and the man was Johnny Diamond. I'll never forget his face.

I remember all this very distinctly. After all it was the biggest thing that had happened to me in years, being an eyewitness to a killing, that is. I'm not about to forget the details of such an experience.

I have read the above statement consisting of two pages, and it is true and correct.


Signed: _Joseph Foster_____     Date: ___12/2/YR-1___
         Joseph Foster


Witness: _Officer Preston_____     Date: ___12/3/YR-1___
        Officer Preston
        Nita City Police Department

# STATEMENT OF ESTELLE MASON[3]

My name is Estelle Mason. I am a waitress at the Truck Stop Cafe, and live at 502 North Allen, Nita City. I am twenty-eight years old and single. I work the day shift at the truck stop. I was there the day Trudi Doyle died.

I begin work at 6:00 a.m., which is the time the night shift ends, and my duties include waiting on customers seated at the counter. On the morning of December 1, YR-1, I arrived on time and waited on my first customer at about 6:15. The customer was Joe Foster, a farmer who comes in several times a week around this time. I took his order for hotcakes and orange juice which he has every day he comes in. There weren't too many people in the cafe at that time. Mr. Foster and one other person were seated at the counter, and there were two or three booths that were occupied. Mr. Foster was sitting at the counter, one seat over from the cash register.

I distinctly remember seeing Officer Diamond seated at a booth not far from the counter. He came in often to pick up another waitress, Trudi Doyle, when her shift was over, so I thought nothing of seeing him seated there.

A little while after I had taken Joe Foster's order (I don't know exactly what time), I saw Officer Diamond hurry past the counter toward the front door. I remember this because he was moving so quickly. I was wiping the counter area near Joe Foster at the time, but looked up to see where Diamond was going so fast. He went through the door to the entrance vestibule where Trudi was. It looked like she had gotten some cigarettes. She had turned from the cigarette machine and was facing inside. I couldn't hear what was being said, but I could see that they were talking and that Trudi was shaking her head "no." I could see her head and shoulders, but I couldn't see her whole body because Officer Diamond was standing in the way. The next thing I knew, Trudi moved toward Diamond, and he made a quick movement. He moved towards her quickly and kind of with a jerk. That's all I could see because his back was to me. Then I heard the sound of two shots which sounded like firecrackers. The shots were very close to one another, no more than a second or two apart. I heard Trudi scream, saw her on the floor, and realized she had been shot. Joe Foster had jumped off his seat, hiding behind a stool, I guess, when he heard the shots.

---

[3]This statement was given to David DeGroff, an investigator for defense counsel, at the Truck Stop Cafe on December 5, YR-1.

I immediately went to the kitchen for help and learned that someone had already called the police. When I returned to the front of the cafe, Officer Diamond was kneeling over Trudi, holding her hand.

The whole incident happened very fast, maybe within seven or eight seconds from the time I saw Officer Diamond rush past me, but it is difficult to determine such timing. I was standing only eight or ten feet from the vestibule where it happened.

I didn't see Trudi's hands. I could only see the upper part of her body, her head and shoulders. Diamond was standing in front of her, and also the lower part of the vestibule is wood for about three or four feet up from the floor. Above that it's all glass.

I did not know Trudi real well since we worked on different shifts, but I usually found her friendly when we did talk for a few moments before I'd begin work. I knew that she was dating Diamond.

I have read the above and it is my statement.

Signed: _Estelle Mason_       Date: ____12/5/YR-1____
        Estelle Mason

Witness: _David DeGroff_       Date: ____12/5/YR-1____
         David DeGroff

# STATEMENT OF JOHN MADDEN[4]

My name is John Madden. I am a police officer in Nita City. I am thirty-two, married, with three children, and live at 481 Olive Street, Nita City. I have been a member of the Nita City Police Department for a little over nine years. I was born and raised in Nita City. I worked in my father's hardware store for a few years after high school before entering the Nita Police Academy at age twenty-two. After successfully completing police training, I became a member of the Nita City Police Department and worked my way up through the ranks until reaching my present position of sergeant.

John Diamond, the defendant, is age thirty-three, and has also lived in Nita City all his life. Although I never met John until he joined the police force last year, I knew who he was, as we were about the same age and went to high school together. I, at that time, knew little about John except for the fact that he had never had any police trouble.

John Diamond became a member of the Nita City Police Department in November, YR-2, after just having completed six years in the Marines and the usual police training. While in the Marines he had become an expert in the use of firearms, and owned a Mauser automatic pistol which he always carried while off duty.

John Diamond attained a commendable record during his short time as a police officer. I was personally aware of his performance and progress since I was responsible for filing detailed quarterly reports on him. John Diamond was competent in all aspects of police work and displayed a good attitude toward his work.

In Nita City, we encourage, but do not require, all police officers to carry a firearm while off duty. This is written right in the Nita City Police Department Duty Manual. Carrying such a weapon enables officers to better carry out their sworn affirmative duty to enforce the law twenty-four hours a day. It has been our experience that unarmed off-duty officers are sometimes unable to effectively fulfill that duty when faced with certain emergency situations.

It is my understanding that Officer Diamond was carrying his off-duty weapon immediately after having resigned from the force on December 1, and that this instrument caused the death of Trudi Doyle less than an hour after he went off duty that day.

---

[4]This statement was given to David DeGroff, an investigator for defense counsel, at John Madden's home on December 6, YR-1.

I am familiar with a Mauser automatic. Several of our officers have such a weapon; also I'm used to carrying that kind of gun myself. It was my practice to carry the gun with the hammer in the uncocked position with a bullet in the firing chamber. In my opinion, this is the best way for a police officer to carry this gun because with a round in the chamber it is ready to be used in case of an emergency. It is also very safe because the safety is on, and the hammer needs to be pulled back.

John Diamond and I both worked the night shift (9:00 p.m.-- 5:30 a.m.). As I was responsible for familiarizing the new men with their duties, John Diamond and I occasionally worked together on an assignment or patrol beat. We became friendly with one another but not to the extent where we socialized outside of work. Also, our outside interests were perhaps divergent, as I am a family man with three children, and he is separated from his wife.

Having worked with Diamond for several months, I got to know him quite well both professionally and personally. He was a good officer and an excellent person to work with. Occasionally we would talk about our personal lives, and I knew that he was married with two children, but he had been separated from his wife and children. His divorce had been pending since January, YR-1. He began dating Trudi Doyle sometime in late September, YR-1, and they had lived together for a couple of months before her death on December 1, YR-1. He seemed so much happier after he met Trudi Doyle. He was excited about life and looking forward to the future. Although I didn't personally know Ms. Doyle, I had seen her a couple of times at the Truck Stop Cafe where she worked as a waitress. That particular diner was a favorite coffee break spot for several police officers.

During the night of November 27, YR-1 (three days before Ms. Doyle was shot), Diamond and I were on patrol car duty together. It was at that time that he first told me of his decision to resign from the police force and move to California. He said that he loved Trudi and wanted to take her to California with him because of her dissatisfaction with Nita City and her depressed state of mind. He then told me about what had happened with Trudi just a day or so before. Apparently Trudi had attempted to commit suicide by taking an overdose of barbiturates, and he arrived home just in time to save her life by inducing vomiting and taking her to the hospital. He also told me that she at one other time had unsuccessfully attempted suicide with aspirin. In order to cure her of her inclination to kill herself and to impress upon her the seriousness of her act, he had pointed his unloaded Mauser at her head after her latest suicide attempt and said, "If anyone is going to kill you, I am." This happened that afternoon when he took her home from the hospital. He was very worried about her depressed condition, and he thought maybe that would shock her out of it and make her realize the seriousness and stark reality of her suicide attempts.

He also told me that Trudi had not yet made up her mind to go to California with him, but that he would leave with or without her because he wanted to get away from life in Nita City.

After his shift ended that night (morning of November 28), Diamond submitted his resignation to become effective December 1, YR-1.

On the day of December 1, Diamond completed his normal shift at 5:30 a.m., and he left his forwarding address with the desk clerk so his paycheck would be sent to him. Ms. Doyle was shot in the Truck Stop Cafe at 6:30 a.m. that morning, but I know little more than that Diamond was present at the scene of the shooting when the police arrived and that he did not resist arrest. I was at home and asleep at the time of the shooting.

I have read the above and it is my statement.

Signed: _John Madden_      Date: _12/6/YR-1_
         John Madden

Witness: _David DeGroff_    Date: _12/6/YR-1_
          David DeGroff

December 3, YR-1

Sgt. E.A. Benbrook
Homicide Division
Nita City Police Department
Nita City, Nita

RE:    Deceased Trudi Doyle
DOD:   12-1-YR-1

Dear Sgt. Benbrook:

   Enclosed is a copy of the autopsy report for Ms. Trudi Doyle.
There were five entry and exit bullet wounds:  entry and exit
wound on the right wrist; two entry wounds and one exit wound on
the upper torso. The path of the bullets in the upper torso were
on a downward angle.  A diagram reconstructing the entry, exit,
and path of the bullets is appended to the autopsy report.

   One bullet was recovered.  It was placed in an evidence
container which was sealed and marked with my initials.  It will
be sent to you by messenger, unless I receive other instructions.

   Generally, my medical background is medical school, general
internship, and residency in pathology at the Nita Medical
Center. I am a board-certified pathologist, and my practice is
limited to pathology.  I completed my residency in YR-7 and have
been board-certified since YR-5.  I am presently a Deputy
Coroner, and I have been with the office since YR-7.

   If either your office or the prosecuting attorney desires
further information in this regard, please contact me.

                          Sincerely,

                          James Pierce MD

                          James Pierce, M.D.
                          Deputy Coroner

JP:ns
Enclosure

NITA
MEDICAL EXAMINER DEPARTMENT

Case Title _In Re Doyle, Nita City Police Department_____

Pathologist __James Pierce, M.D._____ Autopsy No. ___6172___

Physician __Darrow County Coroner, Nita City, Nita_ Hospital No. _NA_

Patient _DOYLE, TRUDI_____ Age _23_ Sex _F_ Race _W_

Date, Hour--Death_12/1/YR-1_ Autopsy _12/1/YR-1, 10 A.M._ M.E. No. _1-2315_

Mortuary __Darrow County Morgue_____

Clinical Data:

At 7:10 a.m. on December 1, YR-1, the Coroner's Office was informed of a shooting death and instructed to proceed to the Truck Stop Cafe in Nita City, Nita, to obtain the body for an autopsy. A woman identified as Trudi Doyle was found in the vestibule of the Truck Stop Cafe. She was dead, and the body was transferred to the county morgue at approximately 7:30 a.m. by Coroner's Office personnel.

I began the post-mortem examination at 10:00 a.m. Lateral and AP X-rays of the chest were taken prior to the autopsy, labelled with the date, autopsy number, and the letters "JP" and then preserved. These were interpreted to show a solitary radiodense foreign body in the region of the right paraspinous musculature.

Officer John Smith (Nita City Police Department) was present during the post-mortem examination.

Post-mortem photographs were taken by Officer Smith and Dr. Pierce.

## DIAGNOSES

1.    Gunshot wound to the right wrist.

2.    Gunshot wound to the right anterior thorax.

3.    Gunshot wound to the left anterior thorax.

## CAUSE OF DEATH

Massive Right Hemothorax Secondary to Gunshot Wounds of the Chest.

ME #1-2315
DOYLE, TRUDI

## POST-MORTEM EXAMINATION

GENERAL EXTERNAL APPEARANCE:  The body is that of a young adult
Caucasian woman who measures 64 inches in length, weighs 120
pounds, and appears to be approximately her stated age.
Post-mortem rigidity is present in the muscles of mastication at
the time of autopsy.  Post-mortem lividity is present posteriorly
and is not fixed.

The arm span (reach) is 64 1/2 inches.

General external appearance of the anterior and posterior thorax,
anterior abdominal wall and flanks is normal.

General external appearance of the extremities is normal.

CLOTHING:  The body was dressed in the following articles of
clothing which were removed without alteration and labelled with
the autopsy number, date, and letters JP:  tan outer coat, yellow
dress, slip, brassiere, panties, nylon stockings, and white flat-
heeled shoes.

The tan outer coat is soaked with liquid and dried blood, and on
each side of the midline of the frontal portion there is an
approximately circular 7 mm. in diameter hole.  The fabric at the
margins of these holes is frayed but not charred, and powder
residue cannot be found at the periphery of these holes with the
unaided eye.

A Timex watch with a damaged metal wrist band is worn on the
decedent's right wrist.  The watch has the correct time, and is
running.

EXTERNAL INJURY:  There is an approximately rectangular 1 x 0.8
cm wound on the external surface of the right wrist, centered at
a point 1 cm medial and 1 cm proximal to the ulnar head.  There
is no evidence of powder deposition, stippling, or burning at the
margins of this wound, but fragments of metal, similar in color
and consistency, were found along the subcutaneous tract.  This
wound is consistent with a gunshot wound of entrance with an
overlying intermediary target, and is designated for purposes of
reference as wound #1.

ME#1-2315
DOYLE, TRUDI

There is a "punched-out", irregularly margined, approximately circular, 9 mm in diameter, wound on the volar surface of the right wrist. There is a 2 mm abrasion collar at the margins of this wound, and no evidence of powder stippling, burning, or soot at the periphery of the wound. This wound is consistent with a shored wound of exit, and is designated as wound #2. The metal wrist band worn by the decedent does not overlie the volar tract of this wound.

There is an approximately circular 7 mm in diameter wound in the skin of the right anterior thorax, centered at a point 15 cm caudad to the manubrial notch and 4.5 cm right lateral to the midline. A concentric 4 mm wide abrasion ring is at the periphery of this wound, and a 1 x 1 mm metallic foreign body, similar in color and consistency to that of the metal wrist band worn by the decedent, is embedded in the skin of the abrasion collar. There is no evidence of soot deposition, stippling, or burning at the margins or subcutaneous depths of this wound, which for purposes of reference is arbitrarily designated as wound #3.

There is an approximately circular 6 mm in diameter wound in the skin of the left anterior thorax, centered at a point 18 cm caudad to the manubrial notch and 5 cm left lateral to the midline. A 2 mm wide abrasion collar is at the margin of this wound, and there is no evidence of burning, stippling, or soot deposition at the periphery or subcutaneous depths of the wound. For purposes of reference, this wound is arbitrarily designated as wound #4.

There is a 1 cm laceration in the skin of the right posterior thorax, centered at a point 24 cm caudad to the lowest crease of the neck and 3 cm right lateral to the midline. There is no evidence of marginal abrasion at the periphery of this wound. This wound is consistent with a gunshot wound of exit and is designated as wound #5.

There are no other external injuries.

ME #1-2315
DOYLE, TRUDI


<u>INTERNAL EXAMINATION</u>:  The subcutaneous fat of the abdomen is 1
to 1.5 cm thick and the subcutaneous fat of the thorax is
approximately 1 cm thick.  Each of the abdominal organs is
present and is located in its normal anatomical situs.  The
peritoneal surfaces are smooth and glistening.  The left
subdiaphragmatic space contains approximately 15 cc of clotted
and nonclotted blood.

The right chest cavity contains approximately 2000 cc of clotted
and nonclotted blood.  The left chest cavity contains
approximately 25 cc of straw colored serous fluid.

<u>INTERNAL INJURY</u>:  A tract is followed from the wound on the
extensor surface of the right wrist through the subcutaneous fat,
interosseous ligament, and tendon of the palmaris longus muscle.
It exits through the wound on the volar surface of the wrist.
Major arteries, veins, and nerves are not involved within the
tract of this wound.

A tract, which for purposes of reference is arbitrarily
designated as tract A, is followed from wound #3 in the right
anterior thorax through the space between the 4th and 5th costal
cartilage, into the pericardial sac and a laceration of the
lateralmost portion of the epicardium of the right ventricle,
through the posterior portion of the pericardial sac and into a
laceration of the artery and bronchus to the medial segment of
the right middle lung lobe, through the parenchyma of the right
middle lobe and into the space between the 7th and 8th ribs
posteriorly, and into the right paraspinous musculature.  A
severely distorted metal projectile is removed from the terminal
point of this tract, and is placed in a labelled bullet envelope.

There is approximately 2000 cc of clotted and nonclotted blood
within the right chest cavity, as described above, and in
addition, there is hemorrhage along the tract of this wound from
the point of entrance in the right anterior thorax to the point
of termination in the right paraspinous musculature.

The trajectory of this tract (A) makes an angle of approximately 5° to a sagittal plane and 15° caudad to a transverse
plane, which is slightly downward when measured from the front to
the back of the decedent.

ME #1-2315
DOYLE, TRUDI

A tract, which for purposes of reference is arbitrarily designated as tract B, is followed from wound #4 in the left anterior thorax through the costal cartilage of the 5th and 6th ribs, through the dome of the left hemidiaphragm and into the inferiormost portion of the pericardial sac without involvement of the heart itself, across the midline and into the dome of the right hemidiaphragm, into the inferiormost portion of the right chest cavity and a 1 x 6 cm laceration of the anterobasal segment of the right lower lung lobe, into a 1 cm wound of the posterior parietal pleura between the 10th and 11th ribs, into the right paraspinous musculature and through the exit wound #5 in the right posterior thorax.

The trajectory of this tract (B) makes an angle of approximately 30° medial to a sagittal plane and 10° caudad to a transverse plane, which is downward and from the left to right when measured from the front to the back of the decedent.

There are no other internal injuries.

RESPIRATORY SYSTEM: The right lung has a mass of 250 grams and is collapsed. The left lung has a mass of 325 grams and is fully expanded. The pulmonary artery segments are normal, except as described above. The segmental and subsegmental bronchi contain approximately 15-20 cc of liquid and dried blood, but are otherwise normal. The parenchyma of the left lung is normal. The cut surfaces of the right lung are normal except for atelectasis.

CARDIOVASCULAR SYSTEM: The heart has a mass of 280 grams. The cardiac valves are thin and pliable and the coronary arteries are free of atheromatous plaque formation.

The laceration of the lateralmost portion of the epicardium of the right ventricle does not communicate with the ventricular cavity. The right ventricular wall is 3 mm thick and the left ventricular wall is 11 mm thick. The myocardium has a uniform red-brown color and is normal.

The thoracic and abdominal portions of the aorta are normal.

HEPATOBILIARY SYSTEM: The gall bladder wall is thin and pliable and the lumen contains approximately 25 cc of green-black bile and no stones. The cystic and common bile ducts are normal.

ME #1-2315
DOYLE, TRUDI

The liver has a mass of 1260 grams. The capsule of the liver is intact, except for the diaphragmatic reflection of the right lobe. The parenchyma is firm and has a uniform tan-brown color.

LYMPHOID SYSTEM: Para-aortic, hilar, and para-tracheal lymph nodes are small and appear normal.

The spleen has a mass of 110 grams. The capsule is intact and the red pulp is firm. Lymphoid tissue is easily discernible and is represented by uniform 0.5 mm in diameter aggregates of gray-white tissue scattered throughout the parenchyma.

PANCREAS AND ADRENALS: The pancreas and adrenals are normal.

GENITOURINARY SYSTEM: Each kidney has a mass of 120 grams. The capsules of the kidneys are intact and the corticomedullary junctions are distinct. The pelves and ureters are normal.

The bladder contains approximately 150 cc of clear yellow urine.

The bladder mucosa is normal.

The fallopian tubes, ovaries, and endometrium are normal. The endometrium is 1-2 mm thick and has a light tan-brown color.

GASTROINTESTINAL SYSTEM: The esophageal and gastric mucosa are intact. The stomach contains approximately 300 cc of incompletely digested particulate food matter.

The small intestine, appendix, and large bowel are normal.

BRAIN AND CENTRAL NERVOUS SYSTEM: The calvarium is of average thickness and there is no evidence of subgaleal, subdural, or subarachnoid hemorrhage.

The brain has a mass of 1280 grams. The gyri of the cerebral hemispheres are normally prominent and the sulci are normally narrow. Serial coronal sections of the cerebrum and serial transverse sections of the cerebellum are normal. The midbrain, pons, and medulla are normal.

NECK STRUCTURES: The hyoid bone and thyroid cartilage are intact.

ME #1-2315
DOYLE, TRUDI

The lobes of the thyroid gland have approximately equal mass, and have a uniform bright red-brown color and a normal firm texture. Parathyroid tissue is difficult to isolate and none is found.

The cervical portion of the esophageal mucosa is normal.

The larynx and main stem bronchi contain aspirated blood, as described above.

## TOXICOLOGY

For purposes of a blood alcohol determination, blood is aspirated from the left atrium of the heart during performance of the post mortem examination. An aliquot of urine, a portion of liver, and the gastric contents are also saved.

## COMMENT

Microscopic examination will not be performed at this time. However, representative portions of each organ will be embedded in paraffin, and will be available for microscopic examination if it becomes necessary at a future date.

ADDENDUM:  The post mortem blood alcohol level is 0.04 grms/dl. Post-mortem vitreous chemistries are within normal limits.

_James Pierce MD_

James Pierce, M.D.
Deputy Coroner
Darrow County
Nita City, Nita  99995

Dictated 12-1-YR-1
Signed 12-3-YR-1

# Office of the Coroner
# Darrow County
# Nita City, Nita 99995

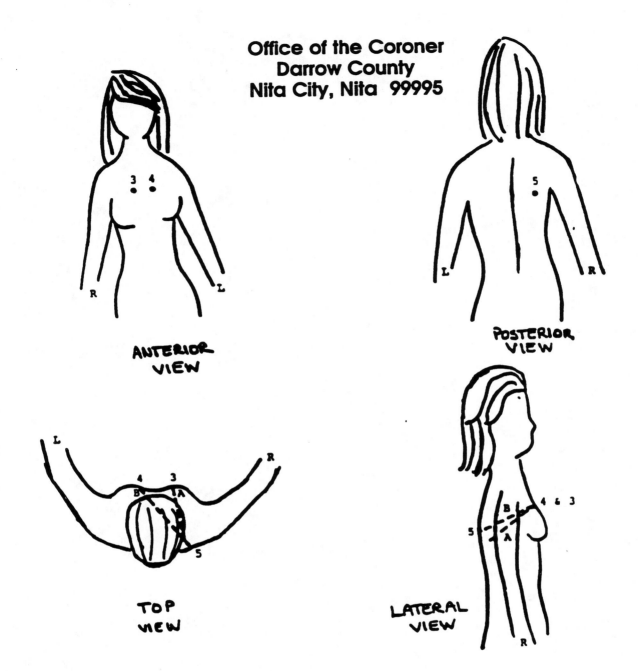

Diagram reconstructing entry, exit, and path of bullets through decedent Trudi Doyle.

James Pierce MD

James Pierce, M.D.
Deputy Coroner

# NITA CITY POLICE DEPARTMENT

## STATEMENT OF JOHN DIAMOND*

This statement was given by John Diamond at the Nita City Police Station between 3:30 and 4:00 p.m. on December 1, YR-1. The statement was transcribed stenographically in the presence of Sgt. E.A. Benbrook, Officer James Anderson, and the shorthand reporter, Donna Williams.

"Yes, I know I've been charged with the first degree murder of my girlfriend, Trudi Doyle.

"I grew up in Nita City, left when I was nineteen and came back in October, YR-2. I am thirty-three years old, married with two children but have been separated from my wife since July, YR-2. My wife has the children. Her divorce action has been pending since January, YR-1. Trudi was twenty-three years old when she died. She was married, had one child, and was also in the process of divorcing her husband from whom she had been separated for eight months.

"I was a police officer with the Nita City Police Force from November, YR-2, to December 1, YR-1. Prior to that I had been in the Marines for 6 years, after having bounced around from job to job with no particular career goals. The Marines really helped to straighten me out in that respect. I got an Honorable Discharge.

"Trudi and I began dating in late September, YR-1, about 2 months before her death. She was a waitress at a highway truck stop and worked the night shift, like I did, so we had a lot of time to spend with each other during the day. I soon found myself falling in love with Trudi. I asked her to marry me as soon as our respective divorces were final. She said she loved me too, but I could never be certain about Trudi's feelings since she was moody and often depressed.

"We lived together at my place for about a month before her death. I knew a lot about judo from my days as a Marine and so spent some time teaching Trudi how to defend herself and how to disarm an assailant. Trudi seemed to really enjoy these lessons,

---

*This statement was taken while the defendant, John Diamond, was in custody on a charge of murder and without having been advised of his right to remain silent and to have an attorney. The statement may not be used by the prosecution during its case-in-chief, but it may be used for impeachment if the defendant testifies. Harris v. New York, 401 U.S. 222 (1971).

treating them almost like games. She particularly enjoyed trying
to snatch my gun from my holster whenever I was armed in her
presence. Because of this I always removed all the bullets from
my pistol when around Trudi so it wouldn't acccidentally
discharge. I constantly carried a gun, whether on or off duty,
since police officers in Nita City are encouraged, though not
required to do so, in order that we might not be helpless in an
emergency situation. I had a Mauser automatic pistol and when
off duty, I carried either it or my service revolver.

"I was also teaching Trudi how to shoot and handle a pistol. I
had become a firearms expert while in the Marines, so was fairly
proficient at giving some lessons. She seemed as fascinated with
this as she was with the judo instructions. As a gift, I gave
her my Mauser automatic pistol, and we always used that gun for
the lessons.

"The reason for the judo and pistol lessons was Trudi's fear
of some truck drivers and salesmen she met daily on her job. She
was a small woman, and was particularly afraid of one truck
driver who used vulgar language and made several passes at her.
I wanted to be sure she could protect herself against punks like
that.

"As I said before, Trudi was often depressed and in fact tried
to kill herself twice. The first time was before I met her. She
had taken a large amount of aspirin but only got sick and had a
'ringing' sensation in her ears. I found out about this only
because of her second attempt on her life which occurred on
November 26, the week before her death. I came home that
afternoon to find that Trudi had taken an overdose of barbiturate
sleeping pills. I force-fed her milk and olive oil, then made
her vomit to get rid of the pills, and rushed her to the
hospital. They pumped her stomach out and held her overnight for
observation.

"I was working the night shift that month. The 26th was my
day off, so I didn't have to go on duty that night. I stayed at
the hospital with her, and it was then that she told me of her
first suicide attempt. I was quite concerned about her suicide
attempts and fearing that she might try something rash again, I
thought it would be better if Trudi did not have the Mauser
pistol I had given her. I remembered that while I was sitting
with Trudi in the hospital that night, I made a mental note to
get the Mauser and put it someplace where she couldn't get to it
if she got depressed again. That night when I left the hospital,
I went home and I immediately got the Mauser and hid it.

"After this incident, I realized how unhappy Trudi was in Nita City, and so the next morning when I saw her at the hospital, I suggested that we both leave for California to start a new life together. She promised to think it over but didn't commit herself at that time.

"Trudi was released from the hospital in the afternoon of November 27, and I took her home. In order to frighten Trudi and make her realize the seriousness of her gestures toward taking her own life, I pointed the Mauser automatic pistol at her head after I brought her home from the hospital, and said, 'If anybody's going to kill you, it will be me.' I then pulled the trigger, but as usual in Trudi's presence, there was no bullet in the chamber.

"When I went to work that night, November 27, I took the Mauser pistol with me and put it in my locker at the police station. I was working the night shift, 9:00 p.m. to 5:30 a.m., and Sgt. John Madden and I were on patrol duty together. I remember relating Trudi's suicide attempts and the incident with the gun to Sgt. Madden, my immediate supervisor, later that night. I also told him of my plans to move to California and marry Trudi, but that I'd leave Nita City without her if she decided not to come with me. After work that night, the morning of November 28, I submitted my resignation to become effective on December 1, three days later.

"On the morning of December 1, I finished my shift at 5:30 as usual, and packed my personal belongings into an airline flight bag. I cleaned out my locker and left my police equipment in the locker. My Mauser pistol was in the locker, and so I tucked it in my pants to take it with me. I never thought about it at the time as I had the habit of carrying it while off duty. I had packed my car the day before, ready to move to California, and I left my forwarding address (that of an old Marine buddy) at the police department, so my paycheck could be forwarded. I saw Sgt. Benbrook briefly on my way out and he wished me luck. I left the police station and went to the Truck Stop Cafe to meet Trudi, who was scheduled to finish her shift at 6:00 a.m.

"When I arrived at the truck stop, I sat in a booth having breakfast and waited for Trudi to come talk with me. She appeared to ignore me, however, and when the shift ended, she sat in a booth at the opposite end of the restaurant with some other waitresses. I was afraid that this was Trudi's way of telling me she didn't want to go to California with me. At 6:30 she got up and headed for the front door. I didn't want her to leave without at least asking her one last time to come with me, and to say goodbye if she refused. I got up quickly, hurrying to the front door. When I got there, she was in the entrance vestibule,

—39—
Diamond Case File

not about to leave but merely using the cigarette machine there. This vestibule was between the door to the street and another door leading into the restaurant area itself. This latter door was glass and shut behind me, so I doubt anyone could hear what was being said. Also, my back was to it so anyone looking in would have a hard time seeing what was happening.

"I told her I was about to leave for California and asked if she'd come with me. She said 'no', and with that she reached for my gun as she had done several times before in our judo lessons. The Mauser was tucked in the front of my pants with the handle sticking out above my belt. It was not in its holster. I knew that I hadn't taken the bullets out of the gun, but the safety was on. Then I saw her release the safety and cock the gun. Fearing that she would shoot me or shoot herself, I struck her arm from underneath to disarm her. This dislodged the gun, and I instinctively reached for it. As I caught it, my finger brushed the trigger causing the gun to discharge. I could see that Trudi was struck in the chest, and being horrified at what had happened, every muscle in my body tensed, including my right hand, causing a second shot to discharge.

"Trudi fell to the ground, and I knelt beside her, holding her hand. She mumbled something inaudible; I told her that I loved her, and I was sorry. The next thing I knew the police arrived, and I went with them without resistance. I didn't talk to the police at first, because I was just too stunned and shocked at what had happened. Later I got a lawyer, and he told me not to say anything to the police.

"The Mauser pistol was not cocked when Trudi grabbed it. That morning I was carrying it in an uncocked position with the hammer down. I had taken it out of my locker to take it with me, and I just tucked it in my belt the way it was in the locker. When Trudi grabbed the gun, she released the safety by sliding it back, and then she cocked the hammer. That is when I acted to try and disarm her. When she cocked it, I got concerned as I didn't know what she was going to do, just horse around, or shoot herself or even me. The gun was loaded, and so I had to do something to get it away from her.

"I can't believe what happened. If only I would have knocked the gun down so it would have been on the floor. This has been a terrible and traumatic experience for me, and I can't talk about it anymore right now."

I hereby certify that this is a true and correct transcription of the statement made by John Diamond on December 1, YR-1, at the Nita City Police Station.

Certified by

*Donna Williams*

DONNA WILLIAMS
Certified Shorthand Reporter (CSR)

| MEMORIAL HOSPITAL | Name First Middle Last | | | | |
|---|---|---|---|---|---|
| **REPORT OF EMERGENCY ROOM TREATMENT NO. 04535** | Trudi Ann Doyle | | | | |

| | | |
|---|---|---|
| | Sex **F** / Age **23** / Date of Admission **11/26/YR-1** | Time Admitted **3:20 pm** / Date of Discharge **11/27/YR-1** / Time Discharged **3:00 pm** |
| | Tel No. **492-3266** | Brought in by **P.O. John Diamond** Relationship |

| Blue Cross # 663392559 | Subscriber's Name Doyle | Medicare No. & Category | Medex No. | Aetna |
|---|---|---|---|---|

| Medicaid No. & Suffix | Our of State Blue Cross Plan -- I.D. No. | Address |
|---|---|---|

| Other Insurance  Address ( ) Group ( ) Individual | Industrial Accident ( ) Yes ( ) No | Employer (Name & Address) | Date of Original Injury |
|---|---|---|---|

| CC | Medical Record Here ☐ Yes ☐ No |
|---|---|

| ALLERGIES: | See Initials |
|---|---|

| Vital Signs B.P.100/55 P. 50 T. 98.6 R. 12 | Name of Doctor Caring for Patient **Troyer** ☐ X-ray ☐ EKG ☒ Lab ☐ Pharm ☐ M & S | Family Doctor **Raycoff** | Nurse's Initials **S.J.** TT BOOSTER ☐ ACE BAND ☐ OSCC ☐ XYLOCAINE |
|---|---|---|---|

HISTORY __Patient swallowed bottle of nembutal. Unknown no. of pills.__
__She had been very depressed the last week.__

EXAM __Patient semi-comatose. Responds poorly to pain stimulae. Voice,__
__speech slurred. Respiration slow and shallow. Pulse poor quality.__
__Temp. normal. No outward sign of head injury. Pupils round,__
__regular, equal.__

TREATMENT __Stomach pumped. Blood barbit. level drawn.__

DIAGNOSIS __Barbiturate poisoning.__

| Disposition of Patient held | Referred to Dr./OPD | DL. | Hospital | Home X | Other | Condition of Patient on Discharge recovered |
|---|---|---|---|---|---|---|

Certified as a true and correct copy of the original in the medical files of Memorial Hospital.

*William F. Coleman*

William Coleman
Medical Records Librarian

Diamond Case File

# DIAGRAM OF MAUSER AUTOMATIC

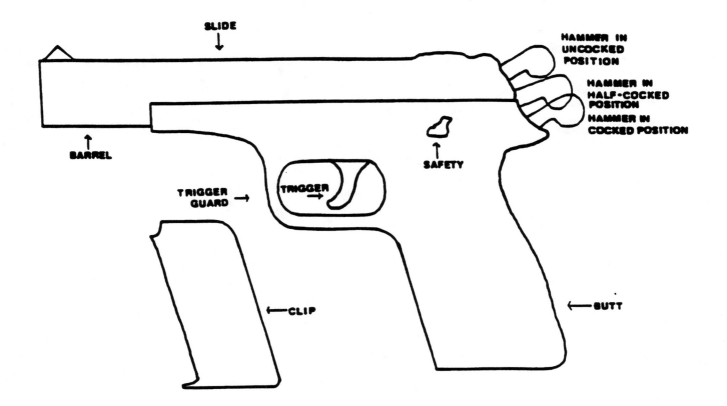

# OPERATION OF MAUSER AUTOMATIC

1.  Bullets are placed in the clip. This model's clip holds nine bullets.

2.  The clip is inserted in the end of the butt of the gun.

3.  A bullet is inserted into the firing chamber. This procedure, called chambering a round, is performed by pulling back and releasing the slide. This also cocks the hammer, thus readying the gun to fire.

4.  When a round is chambered and the hammer cocked, the gun may be placed in an uncocked position by manually moving the hammer slightly back and then slowly forward to the half-cocked or uncocked position, while simultaneously depressing the trigger.

5.  When the clip is loaded and the pistol is fired, the gas behind the exiting bullet forces the slide mechanism back, thus automatically ejecting the spent shell, forcing the hammer back into the cocked position and, while sliding forward again, chambering a new bullet. The pistol is then ready to be fired again by merely pulling the trigger.

6.  Because this gun will not be actually loaded or fired in courtroom demonstrations, the chambering of each round between pulling the trigger must be performed manually, as described in paragraph 3.

7.  The safety is a small catch, which when engaged will prevent the gun from firing even though it is cocked. It must be released manually.

8.  If the trigger is pulled while the hammer is uncocked, the gun will not discharge. The hammer must be manually pulled back to a cocked position before it can be fired.

# APPLICABLE NITA STATUTES

**Nita Criminal Code, Chapter 40.**

## Section 18-3-101. Homicide, Definition of terms.

(1) Homicide means the killing of a person by another.

(2) Person, when referring to the victim of a homicide, means a human being who had been born and was alive at the time of the homicidal act.

(3) The term after deliberation means not only intentionally, but also that the decision to commit the act has been made after the exercise of reflection and judgment concerning the act. An act committed after deliberation is never one which has been committed in a hasty or impulsive manner.

## Section 18-3-102. Murder in the first degree.

(1) A person commits the crime of murder in the first degree if:

> After deliberation and with the intent to cause the death of a person other than himself, he causes the death of that person or of another person.

(2) Murder in the first degree is a class 1 felony.

## Section 18-3-103. Murder in the second degree.

(1) A person commits the crime of murder in the second degree if:

  (a) He intentionally, but not after deliberation, causes the death of a person; or

  (b) With intent to cause serious bodily injury to a person other than himself, he causes the death of that person or of another person.

(2) Diminished responsibility due to lack of mental capacity is not a defense to murder in the second degree.

(3) Murder in the second degree is a class 2 felony.

## Section 18-3-104. Manslaughter.

(1) A person commits the crime of manslaughter if:

  (a) He recklessly causes the death of a person; or

(b) He intentionally, but not after deliberation, causes the death of a person, under circumstances where the act causing the death was performed upon a sudden heat of passion caused by a serious and highly provoking act of the intended victim, affecting the person killing sufficiently to excite an irresistible passion in a reasonable person; but if between the provocation and the killing there is an interval sufficient for the voice of reason and humanity to be heard, the killing is murder.

(2) Manslaughter is a class 4 felony.

## Section 18-3-105.  Criminally negligent homicide.

(1) A person commits the crime of criminally negligent homicide if:

(a) By conduct amounting to criminal negligence, he causes the death of a person;  or

(b) He intentionally causes the death of a person, but he believes in good faith that circumstances exist which would justify the act under Section 18-1-701 and 18-1-702, but his belief that such circumstances exist is unreasonable.

(2) Criminally negligent homicide is a class 1 misdemeanor.

## Section 18-1-105.  Felonies classified, penalties.

Felonies are divided into four classes which are distinguished from one another by the following penalties which are authorized upon conviction:

| Class | Minimum Sentence | Maximum Sentence |
|---|---|---|
| 1 | Fifty years imprisonment | Life imprisonment |
| 2 | Ten years imprisonment | Fifty years imprisonment |
| 3 | Five years imprisonment | Forty years imprisonment |
| 4 | One year imprisonment, or two thousand dollars fine | Ten years imprisonment, or thirty thousand dollars fine, or both |

## Section 18-1-106. Misdemeanors classified, penalties.

Misdemeanors are divided into three classes which are distinguished from one another by the following penalties which are authorized upon conviction:

| Class | Minimum Sentence | Maximum Sentence |
|---|---|---|
| 1 | Twelve months imprisonment, or one thousand dollars fine, or both | Twenty-four months imprisonment, or five thousand dollars fine, or both |
| 2 | Six months imprisonment, or five hundred dollars fine, or both | Twelve months imprisonment, or one thousand dollars fine, or both |
| 3 | Fifty dollars fine | Six months imprisonment, or five hundred dollars fine, or both |

No term of imprisonment for conviction of a misdemeanor shall be served in the state penitentiary unless served concurrently with a term for conviction of a felony.

## Section 18-1-501. Principles of Criminal Culpability, Definitions.

The following definitions are applicable to the determination of culpability requirements for offenses defined in this code:

(1)     Act means a bodily movement, and includes words and possession of property.

(2)     Conduct means an act or omission and its accompanying state of mind or, where relevant, a series of acts or omissions.

(3)     Criminal negligence. A person acts with criminal negligence when, through a gross deviation from the standard of care that a reasonable person would exercise, he fails to perceive a substantial and unjustifiable risk that a result will occur, or that a circumstance exists.

(4)     Culpable mental state means intentionally, or knowingly, or recklessly, or with criminal negligence as these terms are defined in this section.

(5) **Intentionally.** A person acts intentionally with respect to a result or to conduct described by a statute defining an offense when his conscious objective is to cause such result or to engage in such conduct.

(6) **Knowingly.** A person acts knowingly with respect to conduct or to a circumstance described by a statute defining an offense when he is aware that his conduct is of such nature or that such circumstance exists.

(7) **Omission** means a failure to perform an act as to which a duty of performance is imposed by law.

(8) **Recklessly.** A person acts recklessly when he consciously disregards a substantial and unjustifiable risk that a result will occur or that a circumstance exists.

(9) **Voluntary act** means an act performed consciously as a result of effort or determination, and includes the possession of property if the actor was aware of his physical possession or control thereof for a sufficient period to have been able to terminate it.

**Section 18-1-701 and 18-1-702. Justification and Exemption from Criminal Responsibility.**

**Section 18-1-701. Use of Physical Force, Special Relationship.**

The use of physical force upon another person which would otherwise constitute an offense is justifiable and not criminal under any of the following circumstances:

\* \* \*

(4) A person acting under a reasonable belief that another person is about to commit suicide or to inflict serious physical injury upon himself may use reasonable and appropriate physical force upon that person to the extent that it is reasonably necessary to thwart the result.

**Section 18-1-702. Use of Physical Force in Defense of a Person.**

(1) A person is justified in using physical force upon another person in order to defend himself or a third person from what he reasonably believes to be the use or imminent use of unlawful physical force by that other person, and he may use a degree of force which he reasonably believes to be necessary for that purpose.

(2) Deadly physical force may be used only if a person reasonably believes a lesser degree of force is inadequate, and the actor has reasonable ground to believe, and does believe, that he or another person is in imminent danger of being killed or of receiving great bodily harm.

(3)     Notwithstanding the provisions of subsection (1), a person is not justified in using physical force if:

    (a) With intent to cause physical injury or death to another person, he provokes the use of unlawful physical force by that other person;  or

    (b) He is the initial aggressor;  or

    (c) The physical force involved is the product of a combat by agreement not specifically authorized by law.

# APPLICABLE NITA CASE LAW

Justification and Affirmative Defenses. Nita Supreme Court.

   State v. Pierizak, 78 Nita 2d 68 (YR-4). The criminal case law in Nita is well settled that, for affirmative defenses involving principles of justification, the burden of proof is on the State. The defendant has the burden of going forward by raising the defense and presenting some evidence of the defense, but once that is done the burden of proof is on the State to prove each element of the crime charged, including the issue raised by the defense of justification. The term 'affirmative defense' is somewhat misleading because the burden is not on the defendant to prove the defense. Under Section 18-1-606 of the Nita Criminal Code, once the issue of the defense is raised by 'some evidence' that State 'must sustain the burden of proving the defendant guilty beyond a reasonable doubt as to that issue together with all the other elements of the offense'. See also State v. Meninger, 198 Nita 351 (YR-22).

Diamond Case File

# PROPOSED JURY INSTRUCTIONS[5]

1. The court will now instruct you on the law governing this case. You must arrive at your verdict by unanimous vote, applying the law, as you are now instructed, to the facts as you find them to be.

2. The state of Nita has charged the defendant, John Diamond, with the crime of first degree murder, which includes the crimes of second degree murder, manslaughter, and criminally negligent homicide. The defendant has pleaded not guilty.

3. Under the criminal code of the state of Nita, a person commits the crime of first degree murder if, after deliberation and with the intent to cause the death of a person other than himself, he causes the death of that person or of another person.

   Person, when referring to the victim of a homicide, means a human being who had been born and was alive at the time of the homicidal act.

   After deliberation means not only intentionally but also that the decision to commit the act has been made after the exercise of reflection and judgment concerning the act. An act committed after deliberation is never one which has been committed in a hasty or impulsive manner.

4. Under the criminal code of the state of Nita, a person commits the crime of second degree murder if,

   (a) He intentionally, but not after deliberation, causes the death of a person; or

   (b) With intent to cause serious injury to a person other than himself, he causes the death of that person or of another person. Intentionally. A person acts intentionally with respect to a result or to conduct described by a statute defining a crime when his conscious objective is to cause such result or to engage in such conduct.

---

[5]These proposed instructions are those applicable only to this case. For general jury instructions, see those set forth following these instructions.

5. Under the criminal code of the state of Nita, a person commits the crime of manslaughter if,

   (a) He recklessly causes the death of a person; or

   (b) He intentionally, but not after deliberation, causes the death of a person, under circumstances where the act causing the death was performed upon a sudden heat of passion caused by a serious and highly provoking act of the intended victim, but if between the provocation and the killing there is an interval sufficient for the voice of reason and humanity to be heard, the killing is murder.

   Recklessly. A person acts recklessly when he consciously disregards a substantial and unjustifiable risk that a result will occur or that a circumstance exists.

6. Under the criminal code of the state of Nita, a person commits the crime of criminally negligent homicide if,

   (a) By conduct amounting to criminal negligence he causes the death of a person; or

   (b) He intentionally causes the death of a person, but he believes in good faith that circumstances exist which would justify his conduct, but his belief that such circumstances exist is unreasonable.

   Conduct means an act or omission and its accompanying state of mind or, a series of acts or omissions.

   Criminal negligence. A person acts with criminal negligence when, through a gross deviation from the standard of care that a reasonable person would exercise, he fails to perceive a substantial and unjustifiable risk that a result will occur or that a circumstance exists.

7. The use of physical force upon another person is justifiable and not criminal when a person acts under a reasonable belief that another person is about to commit suicide or to inflict serious bodily injury upon himself, and he uses reasonable and appropriate physical force upon that person to the extent that it is reasonably necessary to thwart the result.

8. A person is justified in using physical force upon another person in order to defend himself or a third person from what he reasonably believes to be the use or imminent use of unlawful physical force by that other person, and he may use a degree of force which he reasonably believes to be necessary for that purpose.

However, deadly physical force may be used only if a person reasonably believes a lesser degree of force is inadequate, and the actor has reasonable ground to believe, and does believe, that he or another person is in imminent danger of being killed or of receiving great bodily harm.

9.  To sustain the charge of first degree murder, the state must prove the following propositions:

    (1) That defendant performed the acts which caused the death of Trudi Doyle, a human being; and

    (2) That defendant acted after deliberation and with the intent to cause the death of Trudi Doyle or any other person.

    If you find from your consideration of all the evidence that each of these propositions has been proved beyond a reasonable doubt, then you should find the defendant guilty of first degree murder.

    If, on the other hand, you find from your consideration of all the evidence that either of these propositions has not been proved beyond a reasonable doubt, then you should find the defendant not guilty of first degree murder.

10. To sustain the charge of second degree murder, the State must prove the following propositions:

    (1) That defendant performed the acts which caused the death of Trudi Doyle, a human being; and

    (2) That defendant intended to kill or cause serious bodily injury to Trudi Doyle; and

    (3) That defendant was not justified in using the force which he used.

    If you find from your consideration of all the evidence that each of these propositions has been proved beyond a reasonable doubt, then you should find the defendant guilty of second degree murder.

    If, on the other hand, you find from your consideration of all the evidence that any of these propositions has not been proved beyond a reasonable doubt, then you should find the defendant not guilty of second degree murder.

11. To sustain the charge of manslaughter, the State must prove the following propositions:

   (1) That defendant performed the acts which caused the death of Trudi Doyle, a human being; and

   (2) That defendant acted recklessly; or he acted intentionally, but under a sudden heat of passion caused by a serious and highly provoking action by Trudi Doyle.

   If you find from your consideration of all the evidence that each of these propositions has been proved beyond a reasonable doubt, then you should find the defendant guilty of manslaughter.

   If, on the other hand, you find from your consideration of all the evidence that either of these propositions has not been proved beyond a reasonable doubt, then you should find the defendant not guilty of manslaughter.

12. To sustain the charge of criminally negligent homicide, the State must prove the following propositions:

   (1) That defendant performed the acts which caused the death of Trudi Doyle, a human being, and

   (2) That defendant acted with criminal negligence; or he acted intentionally, but believed in good faith that circumstances existed which would have justified the killing of Trudi Doyle, and defendant's belief that such circumstances existed was unreasonable.

   If you find from your consideration of all the evidence that each of these propositions has been proved beyond a reasonable doubt, then you should find the defendant guilty of criminally negligent homicide.

   If, on the other hand, you find from your consideration of all the evidence that either of these propositions has not been proved beyond a reasonable doubt, then you should find the defendant not guilty of criminally negligent homicide.

13. The unintentional killing of a human being is excusable and not unlawful when committed by accident in the performance of a lawful act by lawful means and where the person causing the death acted with that care and caution which would be exercised by an ordinarily careful and prudent individual under like circumstances.

   If you find that Trudi Doyle lost her life by such an accident, then you should find the defendant not guilty.

14.     When a person commits an act by accident under circumstances that show no evil design, intention, or culpable negligence, he does not thereby commit a crime.

If you find that Trudi Doyle lost her life by such an accident, then you should find the defendant not guilty.

# NITA
# GENERAL JURY INSTRUCTIONS

The following jury instructions are intended for use with any of the files contained in these materials regardless of whether the trial is in Nita state court or in federal court. In addition, each of the files contains special instructions dealing with the law applicable in the particular case. The instructions set forth here state general principles that may be applicable in any of the cases and may be used at the discretion of the trial judge.*

# PART I
# PRELIMINARY INSTRUCTIONS
# GIVEN PRIOR TO THE EVIDENCE
## (For Civil or Criminal Cases)

## Nita Instruction 01:01 — Introduction

You have been selected as jurors and have taken an oath to well and truly try this cause. This trial will last one day.

During the progress of the trial there will be periods of time when the Court recesses. During those periods of time, you must not talk about this case among yourselves or with anyone else.

During the trial, do not talk to any of the parties, their lawyers or any of the witnesses.

If any attempt is made by anyone to talk to you concerning the matters here under consideration, you should immediately report that fact to the Court.

You should keep an open mind. You should not form or express an opinion during the trial and should reach no conclusion in this case until you have heard all of the evidence, the arguments of counsel, and the final instructions as to the law that will be given to you by the Court.

## Nita Instruction 01:02 — Conduct of the Trial

First, the attorneys will have an opportunity to make opening statements. These statements are not evidence and should be considered only as a preview of what the attorneys expect the evidence will be.

---

*The instructions contained in this section are borrowed or adapted from a number of sources including California, Illinois, Indiana, Washington, and Colorado pattern jury instructions.

Following the opening statements, witnesses will be called to testify. They will be placed under oath and questioned by the attorneys. Documents and other tangible exhibits may also be received as evidence. If an exhibit is given to you to examine, you should examine it carefully, individually, and without any comment.

It is counsel's right and duty to object when testimony or other evidence is being offered that he or she believes is not admissible.

When the Court sustains an objection to a question, the jurors must disregard the question and the answer, if one has been given, and draw no inference from the question or answer or speculate as to what the witness would have said if permitted to answer. Jurors must also disregard evidence stricken from the record.

When the Court sustains an objection to any evidence the jurors must disregard that evidence.

When the Court overrules an objection to any evidence, the jurors must not give that evidence any more weight than if the objection had not been made.

When the evidence is completed, the attorneys will make final statements. These final statements are not evidence but are given to assist you in evaluating the evidence. The attorneys are also permitted to argue in an attempt to persuade you to a particular verdict. You may accept or reject those arguments as you see fit.

Finally, just before you retire to consider your verdict, I will give you further instructions on the law that applies to this case.


# PART II
## FINAL INSTRUCTIONS
## GENERAL PRINCIPLES


### General Instructions for Both Civil and Criminal Cases


### Nita Instruction 1:01 — Introduction

Members of the jury, the evidence and arguments in this case have been completed, and I will now instruct you as to the law.

The law applicable to this case is stated in these instructions and it is your duty to follow all of them. You must not single out certain instructions and disregard others.

It is your duty to determine the facts, and to determine them only from the evidence in this case. You are to apply the law to the facts and in this way decide the case. You must not be governed or influenced by sympathy or prejudice for or against any party in this case. Your verdict must be based on evidence and not upon speculation, guess, or conjecture.

From time to time the court has ruled on the admissibility of evidence. You must not concern yourselves with the reasons for these rulings. You should disregard questions and exhibits that were withdrawn or to which objections were sustained.

You should also disregard testimony and exhibits that the court has refused or stricken.

The evidence that you should consider consists only of the witnesses' testimonies and the exhibits the court has received.

Any evidence that was received for a limited purpose should not be considered by you for any other purpose.

You should consider all the evidence in the light of your own observations and experiences in life.

Neither by these instructions nor by any ruling or remark that I have made do I mean to indicate any opinion as to the facts or as to what your verdict should be.

## Nita Instruction 1:02 — Opening Statements and Closing Arguments

Opening statements are made by the attorneys to acquaint you with the facts they expect to prove. Closing arguments are made by the attorneys to discuss the facts and circumstances in the case, and should be confined to the evidence and to reasonable inferences to be drawn therefrom. Neither opening statements nor closing arguments are evidence, and any statement or argument made by the attorneys that is not based on the evidence should be disregarded.

## Nita Instruction 1:03 — Credibility of Witnesses

You are the sole judges of the credibility of the witnesses and of the weight to be given to the testimony of each witness. In determining what credit is to be given any witness, you may take into account his ability and opportunity to observe; his manner and appearance while testifying; any interest, bias, or prejudice he may have; the reasonableness of his testimony considered in the light of all the evidence; and any other factors that bear on the believability and weight of the witness's testimony.

## Nita Instruction 1:04 — Expert Witnesses

You have heard evidence in this case from witnesses who testified as experts. The law allows experts to express an opinion on subjects involving their special knowledge, training and skill, experience, or research. While their opinions are allowed to be given, it is entirely within the province of the jury to determine what weight shall be given their testimony. Jurors are not bound by the testimony of experts; their testimony is to be weighed as that of any other witness.

## Nita Instruction 1:05 — Direct and Circumstantial Evidence

The law recognizes two kinds of evidence: direct and circum-stantial. Direct evidence proves a fact directly; that is, the evidence by itself, if true, establishes the fact. Circumstantial evidence is the proof of facts or circumstances that give rise to a reasonable inference of other facts; that is, circumstantial evidence proves a fact indirectly in that it follows from other facts or circumstances according to common experience and observations in life. An eyewitness is a common example of direct evidence, while human footprints are circumstantial evidence that a person was present.

The law makes no distinction between direct and circumstantial evidence as to the degree or amount of proof required, and each should be considered according to whatever weight or value it may have. All of the evidence should be considered and evaluated by you in arriving at your verdict.

## Nita Instruction 1:06 — Concluding Instruction

The Court did not in any way and does not by these instructions give or intimate any opinions as to what has or has not been proven in the case, or as to what are or are not the facts of the case.

No one of these instructions states all of the law applicable, but all of them must be taken, read, and considered together as they are connected with and related to each other as a whole.

You must not be concerned with the wisdom of any rule of law. Regardless of any opinions you may have as to what the law ought to be, it would be a violation of your sworn duty to base a verdict upon any other view of the law than that given in the instructions of the court.

## General Instructions for Civil Cases Only

### Nita Instruction 2:01 — Burden of Proof

When I say that a party has the burden of proof on any issue, or use the expression "if you find," "if you decide," or "by a preponderance of the evidence," I mean that you must be persuaded from a consideration of all the evidence in the case that the issue in question is more probably true than not true.

Any findings of fact you make must be based on probabilities, not possibilities. It may not be based on surmise, speculation, or conjecture.

### Nita Instruction 2:02 — Corporate Party

One (Both) of the parties in this case is a corporation (are corporations), and it is (they are) entitled to the same fair treatment as an individual would be entitled to under like circumstances, and you should decide the case with the same impartiality you would use in deciding a case between individuals.

# General Instructions for Criminal Cases Only

## Nita Instruction 3:01 — Indictment (Information)

The indictment (information) in this case is the formal method of accusing the defendant of a crime and placing him on trial. It is not any evidence against the defendant and does not create any inference of guilt. The (State) (Government) has the burden of proving beyond a reasonable doubt every essential element of the crime charged in the indictment (information) (or any of the crimes included therein).

## Nita Instruction 3:02 — Burden of Proof

The (State) (Government) has the burden of proving the guilt of the defendant beyond a reasonable doubt, and this burden remains on the (State) (Government) throughout the case. The defendant is not required to prove his innocence.

## Nita Instruction 3:03 — Reasonable Doubt

Reasonable doubt means a doubt based upon reason and common sense that arises from a fair and rational consideration of all the evidence or lack of evidence in the case. It is a doubt that is not a vague, speculative, or imaginary doubt, but such a doubt as would cause reasonable persons to hesitate to act in matters of importance to themselves.

## Nita Instruction 3:04 — Presumption of Innocence

The defendant is presumed to be innocent of the charges against him. This presumption remains with him throughout every stage of the trial and during your deliberations on the verdict. The presumption is not overcome until, from all the evidence in the case, you are convinced beyond a reasonable doubt that the defendant is guilty.

## Nita Instruction 3:05 — Reputation/Character

The defendant has introduced evidence of his character and reputation for (truth and veracity) (being a peaceful and law-abiding citizen) (morality) (chastity) (honesty and integrity) (etc.). This evidence may be sufficient when considered with the other evidence in the case to raise a reasonable doubt of the defendant's guilt. However, if from all the evidence in the case you are satisfied beyond a reasonable doubt of the defendant's guilt, then it is your duty to find him guilty, even though he may have a good reputation for _____.

IN THE CIRCUIT COURT OF
DARROW COUNTY, NITA

THE PEOPLE OF THE STATE OF NITA    )
                                   )
            v.                     )        Case No. CR 1473
                                   )
JOHN DIAMOND,                      )        JURY VERDICT
Defendant.                         )

    We, the Jury, return the following verdict, and each of us
concurs in this verdict:

[Choose the appropriate verdict]

## I.  NOT GUILTY

    We, the Jury, find the defendant, John Diamond, NOT GUILTY.

                            _____
                            Foreperson

## II.  FIRST DEGREE MURDER

    We, the Jury, find the defendant, John Diamond, GUILTY of
Murder in the First Degree.

                            _____
                            Foreperson

## III.  SECOND DEGREE MURDER

    We, the Jury, find the defendant, John Diamond, GUILTY of
Murder in the Second Degree.

                            _____
                            Foreperson

## IV.  MANSLAUGHTER

We, the Jury, find the defendant, John Diamond, GUILTY of Manslaughter.

_____

Foreperson

## V.  CRIMINALLY NEGLIGENT HOMICIDE

We, the Jury, find the defendant, John Diamond, GUILTY of Criminally Negligent Homicide.

_____

Foreperson